FEATURES

EDITORIAL...2

COULDA' BEEN KONG: KING KONG VS. EBIRAH Take a comprehensive look behind the secret history of OPERATION ROBINSON CRUSOE: KING KONG VS. EBIRAH...8

RANKIN/BASS KONG: THE KING KONG SHOW A brief dossier on THE KING KONG SHOW, including a Mini-Episode Guide, a design sketchbook, and a look at the merchandising of the series...14

GODZILLA VS. EBIRAH This comprehensive article covers everything you could want know on EBIRAH, HORROR OF THE DEEP from the direction, to the special effects to the actors (this includes a look at the original Daiyo, Noriko Takahashi, and also the new Shobijin, Pair Bambi)...22

EXCLUSIVE MANGA Exclusive to this edition, take a look at a rare Japanese manga adaptation of the film (just remember, it goes right to left instead of the other way around!)...57

100 SHOT/100 KILLED Jun Fukuda and Akira Takarada's 100 SHOT/100 KILLED films are both finally avaialbe in the U.S., but are they worth watching?...68

THE LOST FILMS FANZINE PRESENTS MOVIE MILESTONES, VOL. 2, #5 SUMMER 2021

EDITOR AND PUBLISHER: JOHN LEMAY/BICEP BOOKS SPECIAL CONSULTANT: KYLE BYRD SPECIAL THANKS TO STEVEN ARCE/YOSHIDRACO

MOVIE MILESTONES IS A SPECIAL MAGAZINE PUBLISHED IN CONJUNCTION WITH THE LOST FILMS FANZINE. THE COPYRIGHTS AND TRADEMARKS OF THE IMAGES FEATURED HEREIN ARE HELD BY THEIR RESPECTIVE OWNERS. MOVIE MILESTONES ACKNOWLEDGES THE RIGHTS OF THE CREATORS AND THE COPYRIGHT HOLDERS OF THE IMAGES THEREIN AND DOES NOT SEEK TO INFRINGE UPON THOSE RIGHTS. IMAGES AND MATERIALS USED HEREIN ARE PUBLICITY IMAGES THAT WERE MADE AVAILABLE FOR MAGAZINE USE AT THE TIME OF THE RESPECTIVE FILMS RELEASES AND ARE USED IN THE INTEREST OF EDUCATION AND PUBLICITY. ARTICLES AND TEXT WITHIN THE MAGAZINE ARE © THEIR RESPECTIVE AUTHORS AND MAY NOT BE REPRINTED WITHOUT PERMISSION. MOVIE MILESTONES IS NOT ASSOCIATED WITH TOHO CO., LTD. COVER IMAGES: EBIRAH, HORROR OF THE DEEP © 1966 TOHO CO., LTD. AND KING KONG ESCAPES © 1967 TOHO CO., LTD. PREMIUM COLOR EDITION CREDITED TO STEVEN ARCE/YOSHIDRACO BASIC COLOR AND BW COVERS COMPOSED BY JOHN LEMAY CONTACT THE EDITOR @ jplemay@plateautel.net

EDITORIAL

As of this writing, there are now well over thirty official Godzilla movies. Not surprisingly, with that many entries, the series boasts a wide variety of styles and story types. And with that also comes a wide variety of fans. Some prefer the thought-provoking, critically acclaimed entries like the original *Godzilla* (1954), or more recently, *Shin Godzilla* (2016). Then you have fans that are all about fun and monster on monster action, people who prefer movies like *Godzilla vs. Megalon* (1973) or *Godzilla: King of the Monsters* (2019). Notably, Godzilla is an outright villain in the former two named films, and an outright hero in the latter two.

I tend to fall somewhere in between these two groups of fans, and perhaps it should come as no surprise that my favorite film in the series is itself between the two categories I just described. 1966's *Godzilla Versus the Sea Monster* (officially dubbed *Ebirah, Horror of the Deep* by Toho) presented the Big G as neither hero nor villain. Godzilla's saving of the human characters was mostly coincidental. In a way, Godzilla was not unlike the protagonist of a Spaghetti Western, an anti-hero with his own agenda that just happened to benefit the little people. Godzilla was also for the first time presented as "cool," for lack of a better word, besting the villains at every turn.

Though for a time *Ebirah* was considered one of the lesser, sillier Godzilla movies, in more recent years it has been reappraised with the respect that it deserves. You see, there are quite a few viewers out there who can barely put up with the "people parts" in Godzilla movies. Usually they involved scientists spouting off jargon or military officials describing some new super weapon, etc. These wordy scenes could at times be boring. *Ebirah* has none of that though, and the "people parts" are just as action filled and entertaining as the "monster parts." It's a through and through action film, in large part thanks to new director Jun Fukuda. As it was, action films were Fukuda's bread and butter for Toho.

In 1965 he had just directed *100 Shot/100 Killed* (*Ironfinger* internationally), a James Bond spoof starring Akira Takarada. It was scored by *Ebirah's* eventual composer, Masaru Sato, and if one watches the film they will notice the similarity between the scores for *100 Shot* and *Ebirah*. Stylistically the two films are also similar, and even feature many of the same actors. While I wouldn't go so far as to call *100 Shot* a companion piece, the stylistic similarities are undeniable. As such, this issue will also shed some light on the film and its sequel: 1968's *100 Shot/100 Killed: Goldeneye*.

Speaking of *100 Shot* sequels, supposedly in 1966 Toho was developing a sequel to be subtitled *Big Duel in the South Seas*. Allegedly, the proposed storyline for the sequel was shelved and integrated into Toho's next monster film instead: *King Kong vs. Ebirah*. That's the other big interest in *Ebirah*: it started off starring King Kong rather than Godzilla. As this magazine is a subsidiary of *The Lost Films Fanzine*, we will be exploring that topic at length in this issue! While I admit that much of this material has been published be-

THE LOST FILMS FANZINE PRESENTS MOVIE MILESTONES #5

fore, I am happy to say that I at least dug up some new nuggets as to the unmade film's background. And, I can finally answer the nagging question: Was Mothra really going to meet King Kong, or did she get added in with Godzilla?

So, with no more ado, I hope you enjoy this 80 page love letter to my favorite Godzilla film!

John LeMay, Summer 2021

WHAT ALMOST WAS...

What EBIRAH, HORROR OF THE DEEP might have looked like had King Kong starred rather than Godzilla. © 1966 TOHO CO., LTD.

WHAT WAS...

While Kong woulda been cool, Godzilla was pretty cool himself in **EBIRAH, HORROR OF THE DEEP!**
© 1966 TOHO CO., LTD.

COULDA' BEEN KONG!

OPERATION ROBINSON CRUSOE: KING KONG VS. EBIRAH

Intended Release Date: December 1966
Script Date: July 13th, 1966

Screenplay by: SHINICHI SEKIZAWA
Proposed Director: JUN FUKUDA
Proposed SPFX Director: SADAMASA ARIKAWA Proposed Monsters: KING KONG, EBIRAH, GIANT CONDOR, MOTHRA

Today it is common knowledge amongst kaiju fans that EBIRAH, HORROR OF THE DEEP originally started off as OPERATION ROBINSON CRUSOE: KING KONG VS. EBIRAH. Harder to pin down, though, are the precise origins of the aborted King Kong solo film, as there are several versions circulating.

Several sources attest Rankin/Bass approached Toho about co-producing a King Kong vehicle together to be based upon their animated *The King Kong Show* (1966). The series was ironically animated by Toho's competitor Toei in Japan but meant for American TV viewers on ABC. When Rankin/Bass has negotiated for the character rights from RKO, they didn't just get the rights to an animated TV series, they also had the right to do one live-action movie. And that's where Toho came in. Supposedly when Toho decided to put Jun Fukuda and Sadamasa Arikawa on the project, Rankin/Bass balked, wanting Ishiro Honda and Eiji Tsuburaya instead. Also, there were no elements from the TV series in the story, so in the next script, Dr. Who, a main villain in the cartoon, and his creation Mechani-Kong were added.

However, other sources say that Toho had been wanting to do their own series of Kong spin-off films set within the world of Godzilla and wrote the *Operation Robinson Crusoe* script on their own. On the one hand, this theory would seem to make more sense because *The King Kong Show* premiered on September 10, 1966, while Shinichi Sekizawa's script for *Operation Robinson Crusoe* had been completed two whole months before the TV series premiered. So, if Toho and Rankin/Bass were in collusion from the get go, then they were planning on the live-action movie before the series had even come out.

Where the Toho spin-off information comes from is Ray Morton's *King Kong: The History of a Movie Icon from Fay Wray to Peter Jackson*. In the book, he wrote:

Following the tremendous success of *Kingu Kongu Tai Gojira*, Toho was eager to produce an entire series of Kong films. To this end, Tomoyuki Tanaka commissioned a new script called Kingu *Kongu Tai Ebirah (King*

KING KONG VS. EBIRAH

A couple of fan made mock-ups combining the Kong suit from KING KONG VS. GODZILLA with the Sea Monster from EBIRAH, HORROR OF THE DEEP. The poster on page opposite was created by Steven Arce/Yoshidraco.
© 1966 TOHO CO., LTD.

Kong Versus Ebirah), in which Kong battles a giant Condor, Mothra (Toho's kaiju moth), and finally a giant shrimp, Ebirah. All of the monster props and costumes were built for the film, including a new Kong suit and a miniature set representing Kong's island home. Tanaka then approached Daniel O'Shea to negotiate the rights, but RKO-General wouldn't grant Toho permission to make a series. Disappointed, Toho asked for permission to make a single film, so that it could at least recoup the cost of its new Kong suit and sets. RKO-General was willing to allow Toho to make a one off, but it did not like Tanaka's proposed script.

According to Morton's account, RKO then set Toho up with Rankin Bass, who was in the market to produce a live-action version of The King Kong Show. However, even elements of this theory don't entirely hold water as supposedly Toho's licensing fee paid to RKO to use Kong in 1962's King Kong vs. Godzilla gave them the rights to the monster for five years, meaning the rights would expire in 1967. Therefore, why RKO would reject the script seems strange if Toho still had legal rights to the giant ape. Furthermore, Toho had almost exercised their right to more Kong movies right away in 1963, when a treatment for what was called Continuation: King Kong vs. Godzilla was penned by Shinichi Sekizawa. The idea was eventually tossed aside, prseumably for being

Concept artwork for the film created many years later for the ENCYCLOPEDIA OF GODZILLA by Hurricane Ryu. © TOHO CO., LTD.

too repetitive of 1962's *King Kong vs. Godzilla*.

What we do know is that in February of 1966, Toho's senior staff manager, Makoto Fujimoto, met with a movie theater owner in Kansai and divulged to him that the New Year's season would see the release of a new King Kong movie. Furthermore, according to *Toho SPFX Movies Complete Works*, action film director Jun Fukuda was approached about a U.S.-Japan untitled King Kong co-production on April 21, 1966.

Quite a few Japanese sources seem to agree, though, that *Operation Robinson Crusoe: King Kong vs. Ebirah* was always a co-production with Rankin/ Bass on the in-development *King Kong Show*. Whatever the case, Toho's idea to simply swap Godzilla for Kong when the script was rejected was a genius one (especially if it's true that the Ebirah suit and Letchi Island miniature sets had already been constructed). This also leads to an intriguing question: before this, what was the seventh Godzilla film going to be?

For certain, in the year 1966, screenwriter Ei Ogawa was writing a proto-version of what eventually became 1970's *Space Amoeba* (aka *Yog - Monster from Space*) called *Giant Monster Assault*. Though Godzilla's Japanese Wikipedia page halfway implies this

THE LOST FILMS FANZINE PRESENTS MOVIE MILESTONES #5

THE UNMADE FILES: CONTINUATION: KING KONG VS. GODZILLA Considering that 1962's KING KONG VS. GODZILLA was one of the most succesful Japanese films ever made, it's no surprise that Toho was thinking of more King Kong movies. Instead of spinning Kong off into his own series, Toho first thought about giving him a rematch with Godzilla. In the story, Kong would be found in Africa where he fights a giant scorpion to defend an orphaned child. The baby is the sole survivor of a Japanese plane crash, and when it's rescued and taken back home Kong follows. The Japanese government revives Godzilla's seemingly dead body (being used as an amusement park attraction!) to fight Kong. The two titans clash yet again, this time in the middle of a volcanic eruption at Mt. Aso. The treatment ended with both beasts encased in lava. © TOHO CO., LTD.

was a Godzilla film, that is not the case, as Godzilla was certainly not in the script. Actually, in November of 1965, Shinichi Sekizawa was writing *Batman vs. Godzilla*, so perhaps this was the planned G-film of 1966 at one point? Or, perhaps Toho was pondering giving Godzilla a rest for the year 1966.

In any case, there are several scenes in *Ebirah, Horror of the Deep*, that give Godzilla odd, Kong-like behavior, chief among them his infatuation with beautiful native girl Daiyo. And, notably, when Godzilla defends Daiyo from the Giant Condor, this was an homage to the scene from the original 1933 *King Kong* where the big ape defends Ann from a

pterodactyl. Another telling detail is the fact that Godzilla is awakened by electricity. In previous entries, electricity was harmful to Godzilla, whereas Kong feeds off of electricity in *King Kong vs. Godzilla*. Godzilla's fight with Mothra, now an ally since 1964's *Ghidorah, the Three Headed Monster*, is also out of place. Lastly, when Godzilla rips off Ebirah's claws and then taunts him with them, it seems reminiscent of Kong fiddling with the dead Tyrannosaurus' jaws in the original 1933 *King Kong*.

Speaking of Ebirah, the beast would have been a menacing opponent for Kong with his sharp pinchers and aquatic advantage. For Godzilla's tough

Japanese tie-in merchandise with THE KING KONG SHOW featuring a giant condor. Coincidence?

hide and familiarity with the water, not to mention his atomic ray, Ebirah makes for one of Godzilla's least exciting opponents. However, since the Ebirah suit had supposedly already been built, a new monster could not be created to battle the Big G. (Though Teruyoshi Nakano, a Toho effects director, has made the comment that Godzilla's foe for this film was to be a giant octopus.)

Ultimately, one has to ask if Toho changed anything at all in the script once Godzilla was swapped for Kong? On that note, some sources have claimed that the only major change to the whole script after Godzilla was swapped in was the scene with the jet fighters so that Godzilla could shoot them down with his radioactive ray. But, this has never been proven as the script for *King Kong vs. Ebirah* has never surfaced, not even in *Toho Tokusatsu Unpublished Works* (it does list the script as being 119 pages though). Perhaps the jets were in the Kong script, and they were an homage to the airplanes from *King Kong* (1933) just like the giant condor?

And for one final question: was Mothra actually in the *King Kong vs. Ebirah* script? If that script was indeed a product of servicing Rankin/Bass's *The King Kong Show* then this would seem to be unlikely. After all, Mothra certainly never popped up on the show. The inclusion of Mothra makes it more likely that the script was a Toho created Kong spin-off with no involvement from Rankin/Bass. For many years, I could find no definitive answer as to Mothra's presence in *King Kong vs. Ebirah*. My best lead for a long time was *Encyclopedia of Godzilla (Mechagodzilla Edition)* from 1993. It lists a synopsis that is exactly the same as *Ebirah, Horror of the Deep*, Mothra and all, only with Kong. This author wonders if that book's compilers were merely making assumptions though.

I also found sources to the contrary that implied that Mothra was added into the film with Godzilla due to a recent poll which found that Mothra was Toho's most popular monster! (Regardless of whether Mothra was added into the film later or not, the business about her being the most popular Toho monster in a poll was true, though).

Finally, I found concrete proof that Mothra and Kong were indeed meant to tangle onscreen via the 30 minute

Though Mothra and Kong may seem like strange bedfellows, the original MOTHRA was itself inspired by the movie KING KONG by Ishiro Honda's own admission in an interview!
© 1966 TOHO CO., LTD.

Still from FATHER OF ULTRA Q
© 1966 TSUBURAYA

TV special *Father of Ultra Q* (aired June 2, 1966). During the program, which served as a behind-the-scenes look at *Ultra Q* and mostly comprised of an interview with Eiji Tsuburaya, the project was brought up. Or, at least that's what I read on *Ebirah's* Japanese Wikipedia page, which stated that Tsuburaya mentioned prepping the new "King Kong and Mothra movie project." (In the same piece Fukuda was announced as director and that Arikawa would handle most of the effects was also confirmed.)

At first, I worried this might be information of a dubious veracity, perhaps the program said no such thing. But, luckily, I found a clip of the program and could clearly hear Tsuburaya say the words "Kingu Kongu and Mosura." This confirms the Mothra story finally after all these years.

While it would've certainly been fun to see Kong gawk at Daiyo, battle Ebirah, and marvel at Mothra, if he had then we would certainly be out one of the more fun Godzilla movies. But still, more Toho Kong movies in the 1960s certainly would have been welcome, and *King Kong Escapes*, produced and released in 1967, is also a wonderful fantasy film.

THE KING KONG SHOW

Airdate:
September 10, 1966-August 31, 1969

In early 1966, Rankin/Bass, the studio behind classics like RUDOLPH, THE RED-NOSED REINDEER, negotiated the rights from RKO to do an animated King Kong series for children along with the rights for one live-action movie based on the series. To do the animation, Rankin/Bass would farm out the process to Toei Studios in Japan, which in addition to live-action films also produced animation. The character designs were still done in America though, notably by Jack Davis and Rod Willis. Of the two, Davis was better known as one of the founders of MAD MAGAZINE, and was known for his odd characterizations, giving figures large heads and small legs (which also applied to his rendition of Kong).

Rankin/Bass decided to do a first with Kong, and portray him as a hero rather than sympathetic villain. Writers Lew Lewis, Bernard Cowan, and Ron Levy then developed a basic premise where Kong would become guardian to a family of scientists. Ties to the film were scarce, swapping Skull Island for Mondo Island. In this iteration Kong never did fall from the Empire State Building. Instead he is discovered by the Bond family, consisting of Professor Bond and his two children, Susan and Bobby, on Mondo Island. The only character to even return from the original 1933 *King Kong* was Captain Englehorn, who escorts the Bond family on their adventures. Kong would spend much of the series battling monsters, mad scientists and assorted bad guys, the only reoccurring one being Dr. Who, who created robots like Mechani-kong and Mecha-Sphynx.

The series premiered with a special one hour block in primetime on September 10, 1966 on ABC. This pilot movie of sorts had the Bonds arriving on Mondo Island with Captain Englehorn. There Kong takes a protective interest in Bobby when he saves him from a T-Rex and is from that point forward considered a hero. Later, Kong also battles a giant octopus, called the Kraken. (This could have been a nod to Kong's battle with an octopus in Toho's *King Kong vs. Godzilla*). Later, a storm carries Kong away from Mondo all the way to New York, where he climbs the Empire State Building. The Bonds arrive and then convince the military not to hurt Kong. (Later, this premier was split into two separate episodes for syndication called "A Friend in Need" and "The Key to the City." Ironically, they were made to be the last episodes of the series in the syndicated version!)

After the special prime time pilot, *The King Kong Show* was moved to Saturday mornings where it belonged with the other cartoons. It was paired with *Tom Of T.H.U.M.B.*, a show about a tiny secret

THE KING KONG SHOW

agent. In Japan, the first two episodes were combined into a 56-minute special, titled *King of the World: The King Kong Show* which aired December 31, 1966. It was then broadcast regularly as *King Kong & 001/7 Tom Thumb*. In all, 25 episodes were produced with its run in the U.S. concluding on August 31, 1969 (though the latter two years were in reruns).

Among the show's more significant storylines were the re-occurring threat of Dr. Who, a bald, bulbous headed man of very short stature. One episode had a military group trying to set up a base on Mondo Island (somewhat similar to the plot of *King Kong vs. Ebirah*). One had the Bonds going to Paris, where Kong fought a gargoyle awakened from suspended animation. Another had them going to Loch Ness where Kong naturally battles Nessie. Other foes for the ape included giant prehistoric sloths, saber-toothed tigers, a giant vulture, giant bees, and aliens, of course.

As covered earlier, at some point Rankin/Bass connected with Toho to begin production on a movie version which resulted in *King Kong Escapes* in 1967. Brought over from the series were Mondo Island, Mechanikong and Dr. Who, though the Bonds were done away with. As in the series, Dr. Who had a secret base in the Arctic, and at one point kidnapped King Kong via helicopters. The film ends with Kong battling Mechanikong atop Tokyo Tower (no trip to New York in this version).

Today, much of *The King Kong Show* might actually be lost. Classic Media released two volumes of the series containing the first eight episodes in 2005. Though cover art for a third volume, seen at right, was created, it was never released.

KING KONG ESCAPES © 1967 TOHO CO., LTD

EPISODE 1 (9/10/1966)
"Under the Volcano"/"For the Last Time, Feller...I'm Not Bait!"/"The Treasure Trap"

EPISODE 2 (9/17/1966)
"The Horror of Mondo Island"/"Hey, That Was A Close One World!"/"Dr. Who"

EPISODE 3 (9/24/1966)
"Rocket Island"/"I Was A 9 1/2 oz. Weakling 'Till One Day..."/"The African Bees"

EPISODE 4 (10/1/1966)
"The Hunter"/"I Was A Starling for the USA!"/"The Space Men"

EPISODE 5 (10/8/1966)
"The Jinx of the Sphinx"/"Cool Nerves and...Steady Hands"/"The Greeneyed Monster"

EPISODE 6 (10/15/1966)
"The Top of the World"/"All Guys from Outer Space are Creeps"/"The Golden Temple"

EPISODE 7 (10/22/1966)
"The Electric Circle"/"Mechanical Granma"/"Mirror of Destruction"

EPISODE 8 (10/29/1966)
"Tiger Tiger"/"The Day We Almost Had It"/"The Vise of Dr. Who"

EPISODE 9 (11/5/1966)
"King Kong's House"/"Tom Makes History"/"MechaniKong"

EPISODE 10 (11/12/1966)
"The Giant Sloths"/"Tom Scores Again"/"The Legend of Loch Ness"

EPISODE 11 (11/19/1966)
"Dr. Bone"/"Blow, Jack, Blow!"/"No Man's Snowman"

EPISODE 12 (11/26/1966)
"The Desert Pirates"/"Tom and the TV Pirates"/"Command Performance"

MINI EPISODE GUIDE

EPISODE 13 (12/3/1966)
"The Sea Surrounds Us"/"The Girl from M.A.D."/"Show Biz"

EPISODE 14 (12/10/1966)
"The Wizard of Overlord"/"Just One of Those Nights"/"Perilous Porpoise"

EPISODE 15 (12/17/1966)
"The Trojan Horse"/"Runt of 1,000 Faces"/"The Man from K.O.N.G."

EPISODE 16 (12/24/1966)
"Caribbean Cruise"/"Hello, Dollies!"/"Diver's Dilemma"

EPISODE 17 (12/31/1966)
"The Great Sun Spots"/"Pardner"/"Kong is Missing"

EPISODE 18 (1/7/1967)
"In the Land of the Giant Trees"/"Beans is Beans"/"Captain Kong"

EPISODE 19 (1/14/1967)
"Statue of Liberty Play"/"What Goes Up..."/"Pandora's Box"

EPISODE 20 (1/21/1967)
"The Thousand Year Knockout"/"Our Man, the Monster"/"Desert City"

EPISODE 21 (1/28/1967)
"Eagle Squadron"/"Never Trust A Clam"/"The Kong of Stone"

EPISODE 22 (2/4/1967)
"Murderer's Maze"/"Drop that Ocean, Feller"/"The Great Gold Strike"

EPISODE 23 (2/11/1967)
"It Wasn't There Again Today"/"Plug that Leak"/"The Mad Whale"

EPISODE 24 (2/18/1967)
"The King Kong Diamond"/"The Scooby"/"Anchors Away"

EPISODE 25 (2/25/1967)
"A Friend in Need"

EPISODE 26 (3/4/1967)
"The Key to the City" - Part 2

DESIGNING KONG

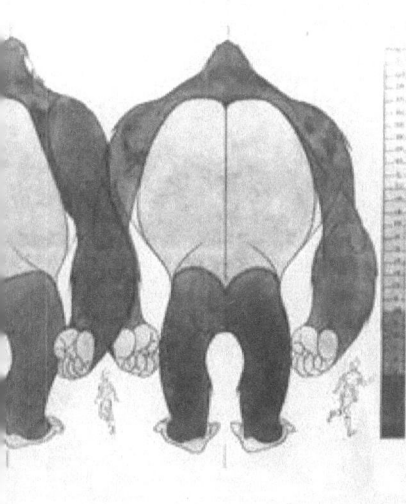

All of the design sketches on this two page spread are close to the final product except for top of page left, which seems to present an alternate design for Kong.

KONG MERCHANDISE

THE KING KONG SHOW produced a wide variety of merchandise in the U.S. and Japan, including toys and games. Japan had several mangas based on the series. In the U.S., Western Comics was in talks with RKO and ABC to license a comic-book of the series but ultimately gave up on the idea.

GODZILLA VS. EBIRAH

TOHO COMPANY presents EBIRAH HORROR OF THE DEEP

EBIRAH, HORROR OF THE DEEP

Release Date: December 17, 1966
Alternate Titles: GODZILLA VERSUS THE SEA MONSTER (U.S.)

DIRECTED BY: Jun Fukuda SPECIAL EFFECTS BY: Eiji Tsuburaya and Sadamasa Arikawa (uncredited) SCREENPLAY BY: Shinichi Sekizawa MUSIC BY: Masaru Sato CAST: Akira Takarada (Yoshimura), Kumi Mizuno (Daiyo), Toru Watanabe (Ryota), Akihiko Hirata (Red Bamboo security commander), Hideo Sunazaki (Nita), Chotaro Togin (Ichino), Toru Ibuki (Yata), Pair Bambi (the Shobijin), Jun Tazaki (Red Bamboo base commander) SUIT PERFORMERS: Haruo Nakajima (Godzilla), Hiroshi Sekita (Ebirah)

Tohoscope, Eastmancolor, 87 Minutes

SYNOPSIS Ryota, a rural youth in search of his shipwrecked brother, sets sail on a stolen yacht with two friends and a bank robber named Yoshimura. The men themselves become shipwrecked on desolate Letchi Island. There they find a terrorist group, the Red Bamboo, in possession of nuclear weapons, a giant mutated lobster that guards the island, a group of enslaved natives from Mothra's Island, and Godzilla slumbering in a cave. The men team up with beautiful slave girl Daiyo to overthrow the soldiers and save the kidnapped islanders. Ryota manages to escape to Mothra's Island via weather balloon where his brother was shipwrecked. Back on Letchi, Yoshimura devises a scheme to wake up Godzilla during a thunderstorm. The beast awakens and goes on a rampage destroying the military base. Ryota and his brother return to Letchi via canoe with instructions from Mothra's fairies for the islanders, freed during Godzilla's attack, to begin constructing a giant net. Evacuating by yacht the soldiers have set the island to self destruct in a nuclear catastrophe. The soldier's yacht is ironically destroyed by their monster Ebirah while escaping. Godzilla then lumbers into the water where he rips the sea monster's claws off sending it in retreat. Mothra then arrives and rescues the castaways grouped together in the giant net moments before the island explodes.

OVERVIEW: As covered earlier, when either RKO or Rankin/Bass balked at the *King Kong vs. Ebirah* script, Toho swapped the monkey for the mutant dinosaur and went on their merry way. One thing Toho didn't keep was the original title: *Operation Robinson Crusoe*. Instead, they titled their new film *Godzilla-Ebirah-Mothra: Big Duel in the South Seas*. Apparently, *Big Duel in the South*

Seas was the subtitle for another unmade Toho film, a sequel to their James Bond inspired *100 Shot/100 Killed* (1965). The film had starred Akira Takarada and was directed by Jun Fukuda, who was not un-coincidentally chosen to direct this film with Takarada in the lead while Ishiro Honda took a break from Godzilla.

As surfer beach movies aimed at teens were also popular at the time, Tanaka insisted the script reflect this, so a trio of youthful heroes was created to start off the film, not un-coincidentally at a jazzy dance-a-thon (though, this creative decision probably dated back to *King Kong vs. Ebirah*). Full of fast paced action, villains lifted straight out of the James Bond series, and water based brawls between the monsters, *Big Duel in the South Seas* made for an all around entertaining feature. Busy with his *Ultraman* TV series, Eiji Tsuburaya let his assistant director, Sadamasa Arikawa take the lion's share of effects work on the new film. Rather than Akira Ifukube, Jun Fukuda insisted that his friend Masaru Sato score the film, making the fresh feel complete.

The film was released as the traditional end of the year blockbuster in December of 1966 following on *War of the Gargantuas* summer release the same year. The attendance dropped from past entries to 3,450, 000, but it was still a less steep drop in attendance than the previous year's effort, *Invasion of Astro Monster*. Considering the lower budget of this picture, it's entirely possible that it was the more profitable of the two.

THE LOST FILMS FANZINE PRESENTS MOVIE MILESTONES #5

Jun Fukuda (man in center pointing) directs the cast. Presumably this still was taken very early on, as the girl playing Daiyo appears to be Noriko Takahashi, who shot a few scenes as the character before fallig ill with appendicitis. See the sidebar on page 46 for more. © 1966 TOHO CO., LTD.

DIRECTION If there are two words commonly used to critique *Ebirah*, they are "colorful" and "fresh" and it's mostly thanks to the new director, Jun Fukuda. Fukuda was born in Manchuria, and got his start at Toho as an assistant director, working on movies like *Rodan* (1956).

In 1959 he directed his first feature *Osorubeki Hiasobi*. However, most tokusatsu fans will cite Fukuda's first film as *Secret of the Telegian* (1960). The film was part of Toho's "Transforming Human Series" that had began with *Invisible Avenger* in 1954. Ishiro Honda was supposed to direct the film, and when he became unavailable Fukuda was pressed into service. To this day, Fukuda cites *Telegian* as the favorite of his sci-fi films. His five Godzilla films, on the other hand, Fukuda has nothing nice to say about, which is a shame because most of them are great. By the early 1960s, Fukuda was Toho's go-to-director for action and crime movies, and had scored a big hit with *100 Shot/100 Killed* (1965). Possibly for this reason, rather than Ishiro Honda, Toho tasked Fukuda with directing their upcoming King Kong movie, and when it switched to Godzilla they kept him on the project.

Fukuda's style on the Godzilla series is decidedly lighter and brighter than Honda's with his films populated with garish colors and comic book style characters. It is said that Fukuda was specifically chosen by Tanaka to mix things up, and Ishiro Honda was never seriously attached to the project. Fukuda did indeed shake things up with a faster paced kinetic formula. The film has been praised by some critics as having one of the strongest human elements of the series, with Stuart Galbraith even stating that were the monsters to be removed it would still be a solid film. As an adventure story this is certainly true as the characters survive a shipwreck only to be stranded on an island with

THE LOST FILMS FANZINE PRESENTS MOVIE MILESTONES #5

Above: Shooting wrap photo for **EBIRAH, HORROR OF THE DEEP.** © 1966 TOHO CO., LTD
Right: Eiji Tsuburaya (left) talks with Jun Fukuda (right).
Bottom: Fukuda working on **GODZILLA VS. MECHA-GODZILLA in 1974.** © 1974 TOHO CO., LTD

an evil military force and giant monsters, giving the plot a great deal of potential for exciting peril. Some of the best scenes of the film involve the castaways breaking in and out of the base. Particularly effective is the film's climax, which possesses an element of suspense that the previous picture, *Invasion of Astro-Monster*, severely lacked. With a nuclear bomb set to destroy the island, the clock is ticking for the natives to build a basket, Mothra to awaken and Godzilla to beat Ebirah and then hightail it out of the area. The editing intercuts all of these sub-plots to some excellent music and the bomb's trigger set to detonate at any moment. All in all, Fukuda's first G-film is arguably his finest, topped only perhaps by his last, *Godzilla vs. Mechagodzilla*, in 1974.

25

THE LOST FILMS FANZINE PRESENTS MOVIE MILESTONES #5

One of the most famous "scenes" from EBIRAH, HORROR OF THE DEEP actually doesn't appear in the movie. The concept art at left shows that there were plans to have Godzilla hoist Ebirah out of the water and swing him by the tail. No such scene was ever filmed, but Toho did stage a series of elaborate publicity stills to help sell the movie. The image was used on numerous posters, and later VHS and DVD releases. (As a kid, I often wondered if it was a deleted scene unique to the Japanese version myself!) On this two page spread are both the stills and behind-the-scenes work to set them up. © 1966 TOHO CO., LTD

26

THE LOST FILMS FANZINE PRESENTS MOVIE MILESTONES #5

Above: Sadamasa Arikawa directs Haruo Nakajima as Godzilla. Right: Filming Godzilla and Ebirah's first battle in the water. EBIRAH, HORROR OF THE DEEP © 1966 TOHO CO., LTD

SPECIAL EFFECTS Although Eiji Tsuburaya is credited as Director of SPFX, truthfully his assistant director Sadamasa Arikawa did the bulk of the work, with Tsuburaya's credit being mostly ceremonial. The work is a notch below *Invasion of Astro Monster's* but considering the film's slightly complicated pre-production process it would be fair to grade the effects on a slight curve. Firstly it must be pointed out that the miniatures were produced for the axed King Kong vehicle, and as such the miniatures were produced with the smaller scale Kong (who stands 35 meters tall in *King Kong Escapes* to Godzilla's traditional 55) in mind, thus Godzilla seems somewhat small and out of scale when he trashes the Red Bamboo Base. Adding insult to injury, the monster's extensive water scenes were filmed first, which horribly warped the suit. As such, Godzilla appears bloated and looks as though he has a hangover during his assault on the Red Bamboo base, which was the last SPFX sequence filmed.

In keeping with Tanaka's "fresh approach" Arikawa tries out a few experimental techniques such as filming the monsters at eye level. A particularly interesting shot occurs when Godzilla fires his ray right into the camera frame, another innovation. The most notable aspect of *Ebirah* is its underwater scenes, which were very dangerous

Above: The massive Mothra marionette makes its last on-screen appearance. Inset: Not an actual scene from the film, but a publicity still.
EBIRAH, HORROR OF THE DEEP © 1966 TOHO

for the suit actors to film. Haruo Nakajima and Hiroshi Sekida had to use off-screen aqualungs to breathe. The shots of Ebirah's claw coming out of the water are particularly well done and creepy making for some of the film's most memorable shots. Arikawa also composes some stunning matte shots involving Mothra and the Shobojin on Infant Island, and particularly when Mothra arrives on Letchi Island as the castaways run to meet her. Speaking of Infant Island, it is a now presented as a tropical paradise with white sandy beaches in a departure from the bitter island scarred by atomic testing in previous entries. This was also likely done because matte paintings from Infant Island in *Mothra vs. Godzilla* of the island's craggy peaks were re-used for Letchi Island, so a change was made to make Infant Island the more friendly of the two. The exploding Letchi Island that closes the film is incredibly well done and would be recycled as stock footage in several other films, notably *Latitude Zero* (1969) and *Godzilla vs. Megalon* (1973).

After this, Arikawa would go on to direct the effects for the next two Godzilla films: 1967's *Son of Godzilla* and 1968's *Destroy All Monsters*. After this, Arikawa would helm the effects of *Yog Monster from Space* (1970), but left Toho shortly afterwards.

THE LOST FILMS FANZINE PRESENTS MOVIE MILESTONES #5

Top left: Masaru Sato. Top Right: Sato and Akira Ifukube. Right: Filming one of the musical Infant Island scenes. EBIRAH, HORROR OF THE DEEP © 1966 TOHO CO., LTD

MUSIC Returning from *Godzilla Raids Again* (1955) is Masaru Sato, second to Akira Ifukube as the greatest (and most frequent) composers of the Godzilla series. He was chosen by Fukuda, who collaborated with Sato quite often.

The score alternates between groovy beach dance tunes, energetic guitar riffs, serene tropical melodies and tense confrontational themes. Ebirah's main theme is an instrumental version of the main song Pair Bambi sings for Mothra. In many ways, Sato's score on *Ebirah* is very similar to his previous collaboration with Fukuda: *100 Shot/100 Killed*. Filled with energetic guitar riffs, the score is more James Bond-like than Godzilla at times. Particularly odd is a rock'n'roll theme devised for Godzilla's attack on the jet fleet, which sounds not unlike the theme to the many "Beach movies" popular at the time. This section of music was wisely cut from the US TV release, but is fun in its own wacky way. Sato's tense music for the climax, intercut with different shots of the action, adds a great deal of suspense to the proceedings.

Sato would go on to score *Son of Godzilla* (1967) and *Godzilla vs. Mechagodzilla* (1974) with Fukuda. In 1973, he notably conducted a grande, poignant score for the mega-hit *Submersion of Japan*.

Godzilla prepping for his big jump, which was one of the movie's better remembered scenes and often re-used as stock footage. EBIRAH, HORROR OF THE DEEP © 1966 TOHO CO., LTD

THE MONSTERS
GODZILLA
(Haruo Nakajima) Making its second major appearance in the series is the 1965 suit that originated in *Invasion of Astro Monster* and was called the DaisensoGoji. Actually, in the time between *Ebirah* and *Invasion*, this suit's head had been "amputated" and placed on the body of the old Mosu-Goji suit for a re-dressed appearance on Eiji Tusburaya's TV series *Ultraman* as the monster Jiras. A new head was then attached to the 1965 suit for the filming of *Ebirah* later in the year.

The suit looks well enough for most of the movie, but the SPFX staff made a huge mistake in not saving the filming of all the water sequences for last. As a result the suit became warped from water damage when it filmed its remaining land sequences, notably the attack on

Godzilla emerges from his cave after a lightning strike revives him.
EBIRAH, HORROR OF THE DEEP © 1966 TOHO CO., LTD

the Red Bamboo Base.

Suits aside, Godzilla's character in the film is something as a milestone. Aware that the monster was now a cultural icon, Toho allowed Godzilla to have several nuances that are comical yet cool at the same time. A good example is when the monster breaks the fourth wall to a degree by scratching his nose in a distinct manner similar to Yuzo Kayama of the *Young Guy* series of films (it was called the "I'm so happy" pose).

The film's most famous scene, perhaps, is a bout of "rock volleyball" that Godzilla and Ebirah engage in during their first battle. Godzilla also has a few odd nuances, such as sleeping in a cave and taking an interest in Kumi Mizuno that can be blamed on King Kong, as these scenes weren't reworked significantly for the altered script featuring Godzilla.

The monster also keeps the upper hand through all of the film, and is rarely bested by Ebirah or the Red Bamboo, his only true foil being Mothra. As Mothra and the islanders leave Godzilla behind, who is unaware of the island's impending doom, they all cheer for him to save himself and make an exit which he does. Godzilla's jump from Letchi Island was done with great aplomb and was recycled in several films and a Cheerio's commercial in the 1980s. All in all this was one of Haruo Nakajima's most challenging, and dangerous, performances as the monster due to the daring underwater sequences.

Despite the damage to the suit, it would nonetheless, be preserved for usage as a water suit in future G-films for the next five years!

GODZILLA IN THE WATER Top of Page: Haruo Nakajima in the Godzilla suit. Above: Godzilla munches on Ebirah. Left: Two behind the scenes stills of the suit underwater. Opposite Page Top: An unused Godzilla puppet does the "I'm so happy" pose. Opposite Page Bottom: This trick shot only makes it appear that Godzilla is underwater. EBIRAH, HORROR OF THE DEEP © 1966 TOHO CO., LTD

THE LOST FILMS FANZINE PRESENTS MOVIE MILESTONES #5

THE LOST FILMS FANZINE PRESENTS MOVIE MILESTONES #5

DAISENSO GOJI (From this page, top, clockwise): Nick Adams and his translator pose with the suit on the set of **INVASION OF ASTRO-MONSTER.** © 1965 TOHO CO., LTD.; DaisensoGoji returns in **SON OF GODZILLA** © 1967 TOHO CO., LTD; the DaisensoGoji's last hurrah: getting sludged by the Smog Monster in **GODZILLA VS. HEDORAH** © 1971 TOHO CO., LTD; the DaisensoGoji prepares to pulverize New York in **DESTROY ALL MONSTERS** © 1968 TOHO CO., LTD; thanks to stock-footage DaisensoGoji has a large role in **GODZILLA'S REVENGE** © 1969 TOHO CO., LTD; the DaisensoGoji head makes an appearance on the famous episode of **ULTRAMAN** (episode #10 "The Mysterious Dinosaur Base") © 1966 TSUBURAYA PRODUCTIONS

37

EBIRAH, HORROR OF THE DEEP © 1966 TOHO

EBIRAH (Hiroshi Sekida) With his sharp pinchers and aquatic advantage, Ebirah would have made for more than a menacing opponent for King Kong. As an opponent for Godzilla following on the heels of the immensely popular King Ghidorah, the monster is severely lacking, however, leaving fans with little doubt that Godzilla can broil his opponent in short order which he more or less does during their first encounter. That being said, Ebirah does provide a true menace to the human cast, several of the extras of which he devours in frightening fashion. He also gets a few good maneuvers in on Godzilla, pulling him under the water a few times and then holding him there, making him a frightening unseen menace when under the water. The monster is thoroughly humiliated by Godzilla in the end, who rips off both his claws and then proceeds to mock Ebirah with them as he swims away in retreat. Although the monster's origins are never explained many speculate he was a lobster (though "ebi" is the Japanese word for shrimp hence Ebirah) mutated by the Red Bamboo's heavy water plant. On the technical side the creature represents one of the more realistic suits of the Toho SPFX department with its glistening wet craggy

hide. Hiroshi Sekida stood waste deep in the water in the Ebirah suit with his legs unseen beneath the waves alongside Haruo Nakajima while a wireworks crew operated the suit's claws. Even though the kaiju gets declawed during the final battle Toho still had plans for reusing him in *Destroy All Monsters* though this never came to fruition. The mammoth lobster does prominently re-appear via stock footage in 1969's *Godzilla's Revenge* and was resurrected for 2004's *Godzilla: Final Wars*. Ebirah should also not be confused with two similar crab monsters called Ganimes that popped up in 1970's *Yog Monster from Space*.

Top: The huge Ebirah claw prop. Inset: Ebirah maquet built in pre-production. According to a Japanese blogger who saw the film as a kid, Ebirah was advertised as" "a monster that sucks radioactive liquid and grows hugely, like a combination of shrimp, scorpions, and crayfish." EBIRAH, HORROR OF THE DEEP © 1966 TOHO CO., LTD

THE LOST FILMS FANZINE PRESENTS MOVIE MILESTONES #5

DESTROY ALL MONSTERS © 1968 TOHO CO., LTD

THE UNMADE FILES: DESTROY ALL MONSTERS Since the initial intentions of DAM were to literally include "all the monsters," the first treatment for the film contained King Kong and Ebirah. As the treatment was considered for a December 1967 release, Kong was still within Toho's rights to use. As such, had it been made, Kong and Ebirah would have shared the screen together after all! However, SON OF GODZILLA was chosen over DAM, which was made in 1968 instead. However, Ebirah was still included for several more drafts. (One source even implied the monster would crawl on land to take part in the final battle!) DESTROY ALL MONSTERS © 1968 TOHO CO., LTD

Though Ebirah didn't make his way into DAM as intended, he did end up in GODZILLA'S REVENGE, though he wasn't scripted to. Originally, new footage of Godzilla battling a giant octopus was to be filmed for the movie. Due to time constraints, the octopus was scrapped and replaced with stock footage of Ebirah. Notably, you can see Ebirah in both the U.S. and Japanese posters for the film. GODZILLA'S REVENGE © 1969 TOHO CO., LTD

40

THE LOST FILMS FANZINE PRESENTS MOVIE MILESTONES #5

EBIRAH, HORROR OF THE DEEP © 1966 TOHO CO., LTD

MOTHRA (marionette) Although her name appears in the Japanese title for marketing reasons, Mothra really only exists in this film as a plot point rather than a full fledged player. As stated earlier, a poll had recently named Mothra Toho's most popular monster, but that didn't mean that Toho would shell out some more money for a new marionette. As it was, the old marionette used in *Mothra vs. Godzilla* (1964) was still in good enough shape for filming -- but just barely.

The prop, by now several years old, was starting to get old and faded looking, particularly the wings, while the Imago's fur is also somewhat dirty looking, Mostly Mothra sits around and sleeps while the natives and the castaways can only hope that she awakens soon. Fukuda gives her a good moment when she finally does awaken, pausing Sato's music as the bug's eyes finally light up and she lets out a loud chirp. Her rescue of the castaways and the Infant Islanders makes for a very exciting climax, and she even engages in a brief tussle with Godzilla who doesn't understand that the island is about to go up in flames. This was the last appearance of the Imago Mothra in the Showa series as presumably the prop had been done away with by the time filming commenced on *Destroy All Monsters*.

41

THE UNMADE FILES: MONSTERS CONVERGE ON OKINAWA: SHOWDOWN IN CAPE ZANPA! Jun Fukuda almost began and ended his kaiju career with Mothra. As it was, 1974's **GODZILLA VS. MECHAGODZILLA** was his last giant monster movie, and it too almost starred the adult Mothra. As originally scripted, Mothra, Godzilla and Anguirus teamed up to fight a giant alien robot called Garugan. Eventually it was decided to make the robot into Mechagodzilla, and Mothra was replaced with the leonine King Seesar based off of Okinawan mythology. (That, and Toho probably didn't want to build an expensive new Mothra marionete, which was more costly and difficult to operate compared to a run-of-the-mill kaiju suit.) **MONSTERS CONVERGE ON OKINAWA** wasn't the only post-**EBIRAH** Showa-era Godzilla movie that Mothra missed. Concept art showed the adult Mothra on Monster Island (along with the Gargantua brothers!) for **GODZILLA'S REVENGE**. The Mothra larva was also supposed to be Godzilla and Anguirus's third teammate in **GODZILLA VS. GIGAN (1972)**.

© TOHO CO., LTD

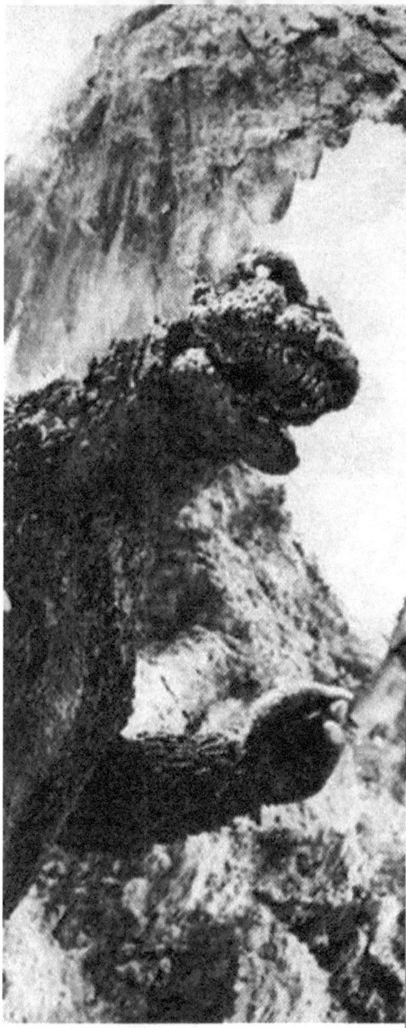

EBIRAH, HORROR OF THE DEEP © 1966 TOHO CO., LTD

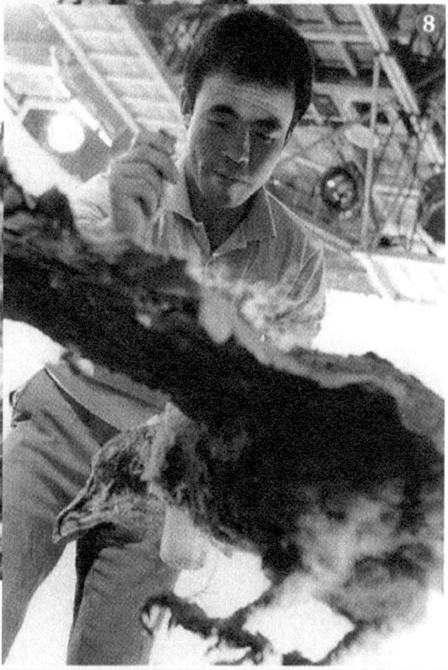

GIANT CONDOR (marionette)

As another minor opponent created to menace King Kong and Daiyo, the giant condor was a decent if ill-executed creation. Many sources attest that it was created from an old Rodan prop (which may have also played Litra in *Ultra Q*), though several fans are skpetical of this claim.

In the film, the bird (which Tomoyuki Tanaka said was mutated by radiation from the Red Bamboo's base) swoops down to menace Godzilla who promptly fries the condor with his breath, sending it careening into the ocean. The creature is on par and not dissimilar to a similar creation in Disney's *In Search of the Castaways*. Like Ebirah, the giant condor would return for *Godzilla's Revenge* in 1969 (though Ichiro identifies it as a giant eagle in that film).

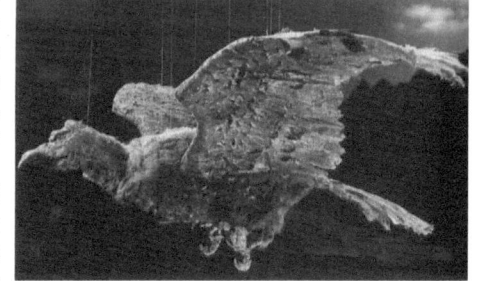

From left to right: Chotaro Togin (Ichino), Hideo Sunazuki (Nita), Akira Takrada (Yoshimura), Kumi Mizuno (Daiyo), Tohru Ibuki (Yata), Toru Watanabe (Ryota) and Pair Bambi (center as Shobijin). Inset: Sneaking into the base.
EBIRAH, HORROR OF THE DEEP © 1966 TOHO CO., LTD

THE CAST

YOSHIMURA (Akira Takarada) Instead of playing a good hearted reporter (*Mothra vs. Godzilla*; 1964), or a patriotic astronaut (*Invasion of Astro-Monster*; 1965), Akira Takadara takes the lead as the ne'er do well bank robber Yoshimura. In the beginning all is going well for Yoshimura, who has stolen some cash and is hiding out on a boat. Ironically enough he finds "his" boat stolen from him when Ryota commandeers it during the night. As a result of Ryota getting him entangled in his own affairs, Yoshimura loses all of the money he stole from the bank when the boat crashes. Once on the island he takes lead of the three youths and helps them to survive and later puts his safe-cracking skills to good use taking down the Red Bamboo, thus redeeming himself. He gets the picture's best laugh when he watches the Red Bamboo from a distance with the other characters and quips, "I don't like to brag, but I always know when I'm being hunted," after which a bullet strikes nearby. By the end of the picture he has decided to go straight completing a satisfying arc for the character.

It's possible Takarada was cast in the film because of his involvement with Jun Fukuda on *100 Shot/100 Killed* though it's never been confirmed. In either case, this would end up being Takarada's last role in the Showa series of films. He would next appear in *Godzilla vs. Mothra* (1992), and then *Godzilla: Final Wars* (2004). That film contains an in-joke regarding *100 Shot/100 Killed* when Takarada's character shoots one of the alien invaders.

DAIYO (Kumi Mizuno) Fan favorite Kumi Mizuno returns from *Invasion of Astro-Monster*, in which she played the tragic Ms. Namikawa, as the innocent but brave island girl Daiyo. Although Mizuno looks sexy as always, she portrays Daiyo so convincingly it's easy to forget her performance as the manipulative Namikawa. Her subtle touches on the character, such as Daiyo's bemusement at all of the smoke bombs, copper wire and other technology, are what make her believable as a character. Dayo meets the castaways when she daringly escapes from the Red Bamboo and joins up with the men in an effort to free the islanders. Daiyo never backs down from the action and gets a noteworthy scene where she interacts with Godzilla, the first actress to ever really do so. All in all Mizuno stands out as one of Godzilla's greatest leading ladies.

This would prove to be Mizuno's last Godzilla movie for many years, but then in 2002 she played the Prime Minister in *Godzilla Against Mechagodzilla*, and returned as a character named Namikawa in *Godzilla: Final Wars* (2004).

Mizuno carved out quite a niche in Toho's fantasy films and is well remembered for roles like Mami, the temptress in *Matango* (1963), Sueko in *Frankenstein Conquers the World* (1965), Akemi in *War of the Gargantuas* (1966), and she even played a butt-kicking ninja in *Whirlwind* (1964).

Kumi Mizuno as Daiyo.
EBIRAH, HORROR OF THE DEEP © 1966 TOHO CO., LTD

THE LOST FILMS FANZINE PRESENTS MOVIE MILESTONES #5

EBIRAH, HORROR OF THE DEEP © 1966 TOHO CO., LTD

THE LOST FILMS FANZINE PRESENTS MOVIE MILESTONES #5

THE GIRL WHO WAS ALMOST DAIYO: Noriko Takahashi was originally cast as Daiyo but developed appendicitis during the first few days of shooting. She was likely cast because she played an island girl in an episode of ULTRA Q the same year in "Fury of the South Seas" featuring a giant octopus. Takahasi also had a small role as a go go girl in FRANKENSTEIN CONQUERS THE WORLD. She was also cast in YOG MONSTER FROM SPACE in a lead female role, but retired from acting shortly before that when she got married. On the opposite page is Takahashi as Daiyo, while this page shows her on ULTRA Q, as well as the giant octopus from the episode.

47

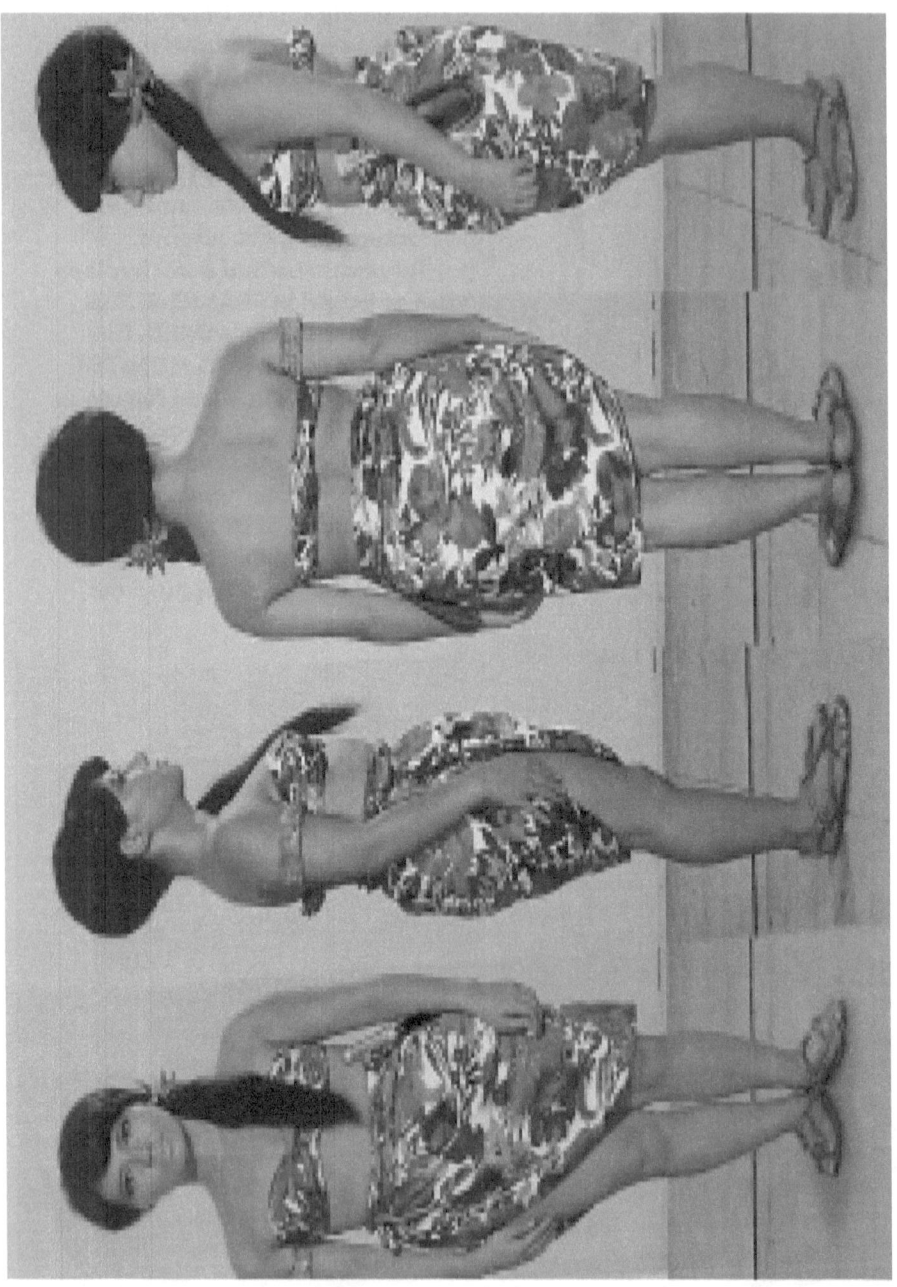

Kumi Mizuno's wardrobe tests for Daiyo. EBIRAH, HORROR OF THE DEEP © 1966 TOHO CO., LTD

THE LOST FILMS FANZINE PRESENTS MOVIE MILESTONES #5

U.K. still for the film featuring Akihiko Hirata's Captain Yamamoto in the background. EBIRAH, HORROR OF THE DEEP © 1966 TOHO CO., LTD

DRAGON SQUAD COMMANDER (Akihiko Hirata) Along with Akira Takarada, Akihiko Hirata was one of the original stars of *Godzilla* (1954) where he played the eye-patch wearing Dr. Serizawa. Here Hirata dons another eye-patch in a rare but delicious turn as a villain known alternately as the Dragon Squad Commander and Captain Yamamoto though neither name is ever spoken in the film. (And yes, the eye-patch was a nod to Serizawa. To emphasize the reversal between good and evil, this time he wears the patch over his left eye rather than his right.)

The character serves as second in command on the island behind the Red Bamboo leader, played by Jun Tazaki, who has a small but intimidating role (frequently only glimpsed on a TV screen). Captain Yamamoto makes an excellent foil to Yoshimura's suave bank robber. It's likely that Hirata was cast because he also played the heavy in *100 Shot/100 Killed* to Takarada's hero. It's also not far fetched to think the eye patch he wears was inspired more so by the Bond villain Largo in *Thunderball* than Serizawa in *Godzilla*.

RYOTA (Toru Watanabe) Although he didn't have Akira Takarada's star power, Tohru Watanabe makes for the heart of the film as the main character Ryota, who is searching for his brother Yata lost at sea. A classic example of a rural youth gone on an adventure to fantastic and mysterious foreign lands, Ryota's unremarkable background makes him an excellent character to anchor the story in reality. Stealing a boat with his two companions who he has just met (a fact lost in the dubbed version) Ryota steals the *Yahlen*, a sailboat said to belong to a rich American. After being stranded on Letchi Island, Ryota learns that his brother was stranded on nearby Infant Island. Ryota does succeed in rescuing his brother when in an adventurous scene he escapes the Red Bamboo via a weather balloon which eventually crashes on Infant Island. The reunited brothers get another exciting scene when they take a boat back to Letchi to rescue their friends only to end up smack dab in the middle of the monster battle. This was Watanabe's only screen credit.

NITA (Hideo Sunazuka) Nita is one of two dance-off contestants roped in by Ryota on his adventure. Although said to be a mountain climber, Nita is fairly cowardly throughout the film, acting as comic relief for the child audience. Captured by the Red Bamboo and thrown in with the Infant Islanders, he does have an important role in defeating his captors as it is his idea to sabotage the yellow liquid that protects the Red Bamboo's vessels. As such, they are killed at the hands of Ebirah. He had many other film roles including an entry of the *Zatochi* series.

ICHINO (Chotaro Togin) As Nita's friend Ichino is Chotaro Togin, who is roped in along with Nita on Ryota's adventure. Ichino's main contribution to the story comes near the middle when he has the idea to wake up Godzilla, who is sleeping in a cave, to wreck havoc on the Red Bamboo.

It's possible that his casting too was as a result of having appeared as Ken in *100 Shot/100 Killed*. This was the first of several appearances in the G-series for Togin, who had a cameo in *Son of Godzilla* and a decent role as a Moonlight SY-3 crewman in *Destroy All Monsters*. He also appeared as a policeman in *Godzilla's Revenge*, and his last role with Toho was 1971's *Battle of Okinawa*.

YATA (Tohru Ibuki) Usually enlisted to play small villainous roles in the background, here Tohru Ibuki gets to play a hero in this film as Yata, the man whom Ryota is searching for, and in a sense the catalyst of the entire plot. Portrayed with conviction by Ibuki, Yata could've have easily fallen into the background once he was rescued, and therefore his purpose in the plot fulfilled, and taken a backseat to the rest of the characters. Instead Yata grabs center stage, rushing ahead "thinking more of others" than himself, as he urges his brother's friends to help rescue the imprisoned natives from the Red Bamboo troops. Later, as time is ticking away to the island's self-destruction in a nuclear blast, Yata remains behind in the Red Bamboo base with his brother Ryota and Yoshimura as they struggle to abort the bomb's countdown. One may argue that the altruistic Yata may have been the catalyst to convince Yoshimura to give up his life of crime. Ibuki would return to the G-series with a prominent villainous role in *Terror of Mechagodzilla* in 1975. He had also starred in *100 Shot 100 Killed* with Takarada, and also *None but the Brave* with Frank Sinatra.

THE SHOBOJIN (Pair Bambi) With Emi and Yumi Ito presumably tired or unable to play the roles for a fourth time, Toho recast the twins with yet another duo of talented twins known as Pair Bambi. Their real names were Yuko and Yoko Okada, born in Nakamura-ku, Nagoya, in April of 1944, making them 22 years-old when appearing in this film.

Although the Peanuts are and always will be the definitive Shobojin, the Ito sisters talents would have been wasted since the fairies are given less to do in this particular outing and have considerably less screen time. Pair Bambi do a good job of filling the Ito sister's shoes and their singing talents are more than adequate.

I have read somewhere, but currently fail to find the source, that Pair Bambi was sometimes an opening act for the Peanuts! Though I can't confirm this, I did at least find quite a few magazines that featured the Peanuts and Pair Bambi together as though they had a professional link to one another. Today, not even Japanese scholars are able to find the old singing duo.

THE LOST FILMS FANZINE PRESENTS MOVIE MILESTONES #5

Top Left: Pair Bambi pose for a publicity still for EBIRAH, HORROR OF THE DEEP. Unlike the Peanuts, Pair Bambi had makeup applied to them to darken their skin and make them appear Polynesian.
EBIRAH, HORROR OF THE DEEP
© 1966 TOHO CO., LTD

Below: The duo as they appeared in real life (notice the Bambi on their sweaters).

51

THE LOST FILMS FANZINE PRESENTS MOVIE MILESTONES #5

THE LOST FILMS FANZINE PRESENTS MOVIE MILESTONES #5

53

THE LOST FILMS FANZINE PRESENTS MOVIE MILESTONES #5

MARKETING AND MERCHADISE

The film's trailer begins excitingly with "Night on Bald Mountain" accompanied by images of the three titular monsters, followed up by a massive nuclear explosion (but not the one actually featured in the film). The rest of the trailer reflects the film's lighter adventure themed tone to yet more classical music. The film's American TV spot is identical to the Japanese trailer only narrated by Hal Linden and cut short by a minute. Oddly enough it was this film's release that coincided with the first Godzilla toys ever produced in Japan. Crude by today's standards, figurines of Godzilla, Mothra and Ebirah were produced by Marusan who finally caught on to the fact that monster toys would sell well with kids. Toys were also made of the previous year's popular Baragon from *Frankenstein Conquers the World*, and also a figure of Gamera from Daiei Studios. Marusan also produced some high end plastic wire control kits for Baragon and Ebirah. The giant shrimp was never popular in terms of figures, nor has Bandai ever produced a mold of the monster for their classic line, so it's a bit ironic that Ebirah was one of the very first monster toys ever produced in Japan. In America, the classic Godzilla Go-Kart model came out at this time.

Above: The first ever Mothra figure, produced in conjunction with the new film in 1966. EBIRAH, HORROR OF THE DEEP © 1966 TOHO CO., LTD

54

THE LOST FILMS FANZINE PRESENTS MOVIE MILESTONES #5

EBIRAH, HORROR OF THE DEEP carries some notoriety as the first Godzilla movie sent straight to television in the U.S. Plans to release GREAT MONSTER WAR (1965) as INVASION OF ASTRO-MONSTER fell through in America—it's release would be delayed until 1970 as MONSTER ZERO. Walter Reade Sterling then acquired the next Godzilla movie for distribution. However, despite GHIDRAH, THE THREE HEADED MONSTER pulling in a nice profit for the same company, they decided not to release EBIRAH, HORROR OF THE DEEP to theaters. And yet, the company still took great care to give the film an excellent English dub (future BARNEY MILLER star Hal Linden even voices Akira Takarada) plus a slight makeover (it excised a few scenes from the opening, namely the credits and a scene of Ryota at a newspaper office, making it four minutes shorter). It was also retitled GODZILLA VERSUS THE SEA MONSTER.

GODZILLA AROUND THE WORLD
Despite its meager reputation, EBIRAH saw a wide international release. It reached Thailand first in 1967, and played theatrically in Britain as EBIRAH, TERROR OF THE DEEP in 1969. It was released in Germany as FRANKENSTEIN AND THE MONSTER FROM THE OCEAN in 1969, in Italy in 1972 as THE RETURN OF GODZILLA (ironically marketed as a King Kong movie!), Spain in 1975 as MONSTERS FROM THE SEA, and GODZILLA VS. THE TERROR OF THE SEAS in Mexico. In 1978 the film was EBIRAH, MONSTER OF MAGIC in Poland and featured a misleading Spanish Galleon about to be swallowed by Godzilla on its poster. It received a very belated theatrical release in France in 1981, and a surprise rerelease in Thailand in 1978 and 1989. The film's strangest foreign title has to be MOTHRA: THE FLYING DRACULA MONSTER for its showing in Holland.

55

In the early 1970s, Toho would often rerelease edited down versions of past SPFX films for their Champion Festival for children, which included EBIRAH. It was cut from 87 minutes to 74 minutes. Supposedly Ishiro Honda did the edit even though it was Fukuda who directed the film. The rerelease garnered 760,000 admissions when released on July 22, 1972. The feature was shown along with an episode of Tsuburaya's superhero series MIRRORMAN, plus four cartoon shorts. To help promote the release, a few new songs were recorded by Masato Shimon and released via Toho Records. The songs included "Godzilla's Bride" and "Rock, Rock Godzilla."

30 ここは、インファント島。今、目ざめたモスラを抱きしめた小美人は、レッチ島をめざしてモスラに乗った小美人は、レッチ島を目ざした。モスラは、ふわりと空中にうかぶと、巨大なつばさをはげしくはばたかせた。

31 ウォーッ
ゴジラは、ついにエビラのはさみをもぎとった。
さすがのエビラも、あわてて海中へにげた。
「あっ、ゴジラがくるぞ。」
「あと三分で爆発だ。」
「早くあみにはいれ。」
「ああ、モスラはまだか。」

32 キューン
とのとき、音より速いモスラが、きっとまいおりてくると、あみをつかんだ。
ウォーッ
えものをとられたゴジラは、上空へむけ放射線を発射した。
「おうい、ゴジラ。早くにげないと、島が爆発するぞう。」

33 ドドド！ レッチ島から火柱があがり、けむりが消えたあとには、島のすがたはなかった。
モスラにはこばれ、インファント島に帰る良太たちは、はるかなる海上を、ぶじに泳いでいくゴジラがいたのに気づかなかった。

〔おわり〕

27 ひみつ工場から、ふじにのがれてきた人々が、がけの上まできたとき、弥太が大声でさけんだ。
「さあ、みんな、この島は、あと五十分でふっとんでしまう。だがその前に、きっとモスラが助けにくる。いそいで大あみを作ろう」

28 ひみつ工場の生きのこりの警備兵は、あわてて船に乗り、島をはなれようとした。たちまちおそうエビラ。
「エビラよりの黄色い水を、どんどんまけ」

だが、エビラは、へいきで近づき、船をうちくだいた。
「やったぞ。あの黄色い水は、われわれが作ったにせ物だ」
仁田と原住民たちは、どっと歓声をあげた。

29 このさわぎに気づいたゴジラは、またもエビラにせまる。たがいににらみあい、すきを見てはがっとぶつかりあう。
「おい、あと十五分しかないぞ」
「あみも、もうできたが、はたしてモスラはきてくれるだろうか」
インファント島の原住民は、いっせいにモスラのいのりをとなえた。

24

良太たちは、ゴジラのおかげで命びろいした。吉村たちとあうことができた。
「あっ、ゴジラが、ひみつ工場のほうへいくわ」
ドヨがさけんだ。
「よし、ぼくたちもいこうよ。そして、みんなをすくうんだ」
良太がさけんだ。

25

ひみつ工場は、ゴジラの攻撃にあって、めちゃめちゃにこわされていた。
警備隊が、やたらに大砲や高圧電線の攻撃をしかけたので、ゴジラはすっかりおこってしまったのだ。
あとかたもなくくずれおちた建物のかげを、地下室のほうへ走っていくのは、吉村と弥太だった。
「さあ、みんなにげるんだ」
吉村は、とくいの錠やぶりで工場の鉄のとびらをあけた。
「おっ、吉村さん」
仁田がまっ先にとびだした。
「ああ、ヤタ、ヤタじゃないか」
原住民たちもとびだした。

26

「ひいっ、ひひひひ」
とつぜん、工場のすみから、くるったような声がきこえた。
吉村が近よると、たおれた建物の下じきになった艦尉隊長だった。
「わしは死ぬ。だが、死ぬのはおれだけじゃない。一時間後、この島は核爆発で消えてしまう。いま、そのボタンをおしたんだ。ひひひ」
こうして、艦尉は息たえた。

22 ぴかぴかっ！　岩山の頭上にいなずまが走る。
ウォーッ
おそろしいほえ声。ねむっていたゴジラが、岩山をまっ二つにしておきあがったのだ。
「やったぞ。避雷針がわりに使ってゴジラの頭に落雷させ、目をさまさせたのだ」
市野がとくいそうにいった。

23 「あっ、ゴジラがエビラを見つけたぞ」
良太兄弟をおって、エビラが、海べの近くまでおそってきたのだ。
ウォーッ
ギューッ
まもなく、レッチ島をゆるがせて、エビラ対ゴジラの、すさまじい大決闘がはじまった。
はさみをふりたてて、あいてのくびをねらうエビラ。それをかわして、エビラを海面にたたきつけるゴジラ……。
グェーッ
さすがのエビラも、すさまじいゴジラの攻撃にあい、ぶきみな音をのこして海中にきえた。

18 ゴジラのねむるほらあなへ命からがらもどったのは、吉村とダヨと市野の三人だった。
「仁田のやつ、ひどいめにあっているだろうな」
「しっ、敵がくる」
「良太だって、どうなっているか」
下の岩を、艦隊たちがくる。
「そうだ。ゴジラをおこして、やつらをやっつけましょう」
市野が名案を思いついた。

19 いっぽう、仁田は、原住民たちのいる工場に入れられた。
「あのう、ぼく、ダヨと友だちだ」
「はんとか、ダヨはどうしてる」
「元気で、ぼくのなかまといるよ」
仁田を信用した原住民たちは、この工場での仕事のことを話した。エビラよけの黄色い液体を作られているのか。ようし、ぼくにいい考えがある。

20 それから数日……。
鏡のようなインファント島にふりそそいだ。
大あれにあれていた。
そのあら波に、木の葉のようにもまれながら、島にこぎよせる小船があった。
「にいちゃん、エビラよけの黄色い水を入れたたるが流された」
「えっ、そいつはまずいぞ」

21 気球でインファント島にまいおりた良太が、兄とめぐりあい、ふたたびレッチ島にもどってきたのだ。
はげしいかみなりが鳴る。
「あっ、にいちゃん、エビラだ」
「あぶない! とびこめ」
つぎのしゅんかん、エビラのはさみが、小船をたたきつぶした。

15
「まて。きまらのことは、レーダーでしっていたぞ」
工場の出口に龍尉が立ちはだかった。
しゅんかん、吉村のあいずで、四人はいっせいに小型爆弾を投げつけた。きっと武器庫から持ちだしてきたのだ。
ババーン　もうもうとあがるけむり。
「このまに、にげろ！」吉村がさけぶ。

16
ウウーッ　ウウーッ
基地じゅうに、けたたましいサイレンが鳴りわたる。
「にがすな。うち殺せ」
小型爆弾で負傷した龍尉は、おにのような顔でどなる。
一行は、さくをやぶってにげたが、良太だけは、ロープに足をとられてころんでしまった。
ダダダダッ
機関銃弾が良太に集中する。

17
「あぁっ」
良太のからだが、ロープにさかさづりにされ、あっというまに、二十メートルもつりあがった。
良太の足にからまったのは、偵察気球のロープだったのだ。機関銃の弾丸で、気球をささえていたロープがきれ、良太が宙づりにされたのだ。
「お、おれもつれていけ」
仁田が、ロープにとびついた。
「くそっ、にがすものか」
龍尉の拳銃が火をふき、ロープに命中した。仁田のからだは地面にたたきつけられた。

11 ダヨの話はつづく。
「わたしたちは、この島の地下工場で働かされています。にげなければ鉄でうたれ、島をぬけ出しても、エビラにおそわれます。」
「ああ、あのばけものえびか」
「モスラにたすけをもとめたのですが、返じようもありません。」
「よし。こっちから攻撃しようぜ」
射たちをやっつけようぜ」
吉村のことばに、良太も、市野も、仁田も、みんなきんせいした。

12 一行が、ほらあなを出ようとしたときだ。
「あっ、吉村さん。あれは?」
良太の指さすほうを見た一行は、思わず息をのんだ。
「ゴ、ゴジラだ……」
大岩のように見えていたのは、よく見ると、いま冬眠中の巨大な怪獣の頭だったのだ。
「そっと出よう。いもぐんだ」

13 ことは、ひみつの地下工場。吉村たちの一行は、とこまでしのびこんできた。
「すげえ、なんの工場だろう」
吉村は、かべにとりつけられたダイヤルに、指をのばした。
吉村がしばらくいじくっていると、やがて、ピーンとかすかな音がした。
「あいたぞ……」
吉村は、とくいそうにいった。

14 「よし、おれが見てくる」
市野が先にはいっていったが、あわてもどってきた。
「もどれもどれ。たいへんだぜ。ここは、核爆弾を作っているひみつ工場だ」
「なに、そりゃまずいな。この場は、いちおうひきあげよう」
さすがの吉村もあわてている。一行は、機械のかげをはうようにして、へやをにげだした。

7

「見たか！ おまえらにげようとしても、エビラのえさになるだけだぞ。さあ、こいつらをつれていけ」

艦尉は、部下に命令した。銃口をつきつけられて、原住民たちは建物へはいっていった。

「艦尉隊長、原住民の女がにげたとの報告です」

「なに、すぐおいかけるんだ」

8

女は、森のおくへにげこんだ。

探索気球からの無電で、艦尉隊はじりじりとグヨをおいつめた。

ダーン ダーン 銃弾がグヨの足をかすめる。

9

「あの女をたすけてやろう」

「うん、女をたしげみの中で、吉村さんは、ぼくもてつだうよ」

良太ははずんだ声でいった。

「おい、こっちへにげるんだ」

吉村は、にげてきたグヨの手をとると、熊山のほらあなのほうへかけだした。グヨのすがたを見うしなった艦尉と部下たちは、あきらめてひきあげた。

10

ほらあなの中で、なにかにのっていたグヨが、いった。

「モスラって…。」「じゃ、きみはインファント島の人！？ よく日本語がわかるね」

吉村が、身を乗りだしてきいた。

「島にいる、ヤタという名の日本人の新聞からならいました」

「ヤタだって、きっと赤太にいさんのことだ」

良太はおどりあがった。

(271)

④
小さな入り江のさんばしに、貨物船が横づけされ、まわりの海面いったいに、黄色い水がまきちらされている。
銃口をつきつけられて、貨物船からおろされたのは、原住民の一団だ。そして、赤い竹づつのようなものが貨物船につみこまれる。
「船長、烈一号三個、おわたしします」
「艦尉、烈一号三個、たしかにうけとった」
将校と船長が、うけわたしをすませた。
と、そのときだ。五人の原住民たちが、とつぜん浜づたいにげだした。

⑤
ダダダダッ！
監視塔の機関銃が火をふいた。
「ぎゃあ……」「うわあ……」「ううっ」
ばたばたと、三人がたおされた。のこったふたりは、むちゅうでカヌーにとびのった。
追いうちをかける警備隊。だが、浜べまでおってきた龍尉は、なにを思ったか、
「うつのをやめろ。ふふふ、いまに見ろよ！」
ぶきみにわらって、カヌーを見送った。

⑥
ザザーッ ザザザーッ
カヌーの前方が、きゅうに波だったと思うと、ガチッガチッと、巨大な二つのはさみがせり出してきた。さらに頭が……むねが……。
全長四十メートルもあろうかと思われる大えびだった。巨大なはさみでカヌーをたたきつぶし、海におちたふたりにおそいかかった。
「エビラ……エビラだ」
海べで見ていた原住民たちは、大さわぎだ。このさわぎのすきに、原住民の女ダヨが、さっとさくをくぐりぬけて、密林ににげこんだ。

映画物語

構成と絵・南村喬之（東宝映画より）

★ ウォーッ　グアーッ
南海をゆるがす、ゴジラ・エビラ・モスラの死闘！

1
ザザッ　ザザーッ
とつぜん海上にあらわれた巨大なはさみ！
「ひゃあ、こっちへくるぞ」
「わあっ、もうだめだ」
バリバリバリッ
巨大なはさみは、あっというまに、ヨット「ヤーレン号」をへしおってしまった。乗っていた四人の

2
そのよく朝……。
日本を遠くはなれた南海の孤島レッチ島の海岸に、四人のわか者がうちあげられていた。
「う、ううむ……」
ひとりが意識をとりもどすと、ほかの三人も、つぎつぎに気がついてきあがった。
「たすかったぞ。おれたちは生きていたんだ」

別冊少年マガジン

100 SHOT/100 KILLED

100 SHOT/100 KILLED

Release Date: December 5, 1965
Alternate Titles: IRONFINGER (International)

DIRECTED BY: Jun Fukuda **SCREENPLAY BY:** Michio Tsuzuki, Kihachi Okamoto **MUSIC BY:** Masaru Sato **CAST:** Akira Takarada (Andrew Hoshino), Mie Hama (Yumi Sawada), Akihiko Hirata (Komori), Ichiro Arishima (Detective Tezuka), Toru Ibuki (Matsuki), Susumu Kurobe (man in sunglasses), Chôtarô Tôgin (Ken)

Tohoscope, Eastmancolor, 93 Minutes

SYNOPSIS A bumbling Japanese man raised in France is en route to see his homeland for the very first time. He befriends a fellow Japanese (really an undercover operative), who is assassinated on a layover in Hong Kong. The man takes on the dead operative's name, Andrew Hoshino, and continues on to Japan. There "Hoshino" is immediately caught in between two warring gangs: the Akatsuki family and Aonuma, who are vying for control of smuggled CRS guns from an arms dealer named Du Bois. Eventually, Hoshino teams up with an explosives expert, Yumi Sawada, who is working for the Akatsuki family, but she switches sides to begin working with Hoshino. Eventually, with the help of Detective Tezuka, Hoshino and Yumi track down Du Bois to the Philippines and bring his operation to an end.

OVERVIEW: Many people have drawn comparisons between the Red Bamboo in *Ebirah, Horror of the Deep* and the James Bond series. They have also noted that *Ebirah* had more so of an action-adventure feel to it than previous Godzilla movies. And though it's tempting to say that James Bond was the direct influence on *Ebirah's* villains and action, the real influence was Jun Fukuda's 1965 actioner *100 Shot/100 Killed*. That film was inspired by the Bond films, and was even titled *Ironfinger* internationally! (That title has absolutely nothing to do with the movie's plot, and seems to be a self-aware nod to the fact that it was a Bond knock-off. But on the same note, nor does Takarada shoot 100 people over the course of the film).

If you watch *100 Shot* with *Ebirah* in mind, you can definitely look at it as a stylistic precursor in many ways—it even has most of the same cast. Chotaro Togin and Tohru Ibuki have roles as minor villains (as does *Ultraman's* Susumu Kurobe for that matter). Akihiko Hirata serves the role of deadly henchman/second in command to the main villain common to the Bond movies (his method of disposal is tossing acid on his victims).

Fans will also notice that Masaru Sato's music for *100 Shot* preceded similar compositions for *Ebirah*, even using many of the same unique instruments. Fukuda's direction and the zany style of the action is also naturally similar to *Ebirah*. The climax even takes place on a tropical island.

In terms of how it relates to the Bond films, it has a pre-credit action scene followed by a title song sequence (though neither are as elaborate as the Bond films). Takarada's Hoshino character really isn't much like Bond at all though, as he's a bit of a bumbler who speaks often of his mother (though this is likely just an act). As it is, if one isn't paying close attention, it's easy to misinterpret who "Andrew Hoshino" really is. Without giving the film your complete attention you might walk away thinking Hoshino really was just a tourist with an uncanny ability to get himself into and out of trouble. But, watching closely you realize that Takarada's character starts out the film unnamed. Andrew Hoshino is the name of the Japanese agent killed early on in the picture. Furthermore, Takarada is only pretending to be a bumbling tourist, he's really shadowing the agent. For the film's first few minutes, we are actually fooled into thinking he is a bumbling tourist. But, when he manages to hit the assassin on the motorcycle in only one shot we know there's got to be more to him than meets the eye. By the end of the film we may not know if he really was an INTERPOL agent or a hitman, but we know that he's not the bumbling momma's boy (we don't ever meet the aforementioned mother, either).

Takarada has great timing as Hoshino, particularly when he's being a momma's boy. A particularly good scene has Hoshino, bound and unconscious after being kidnapped, suddenly shouting "Momma!" the moment he wakes. Chotaro Togin plays a thug holding him at gunpoint, and Hoshino puts on a good act for him, claiming that his partners "008, 009 and 010" will be arriving to save him soon. This is all just to keep the thug preoccupied while Hoshino uses a special wristwatch with a knife in it to cut the ropes binding his hands. As for Hoshino's other memorable scenes, one has him beating a thug with a toilet plunger in a grungy bathroom!

More interesting than Hoshino is Mie Hama's character, Yumi, who is more of a Bond girl in this film than Hama's character was in *You Only Live Twice* (1967)! In that film, she doesn't appear until late in the story (relatively speaking) and spends the remainder as little more than eye candy. Yumi is an independent operator, specifically an expert in explosives. She is particularly adept at setting off plastic explosives with a supersonic whistle, disguised as a necklace around her neck. Actually, rather than a sequel focusing on Hoshino, a sequel starring Hama as Yumi might have been more fun.

Speaking of *You Only Live Twice*, that film contained a scene where Bond was left handcuffed in an out of control airplane when the pilot jumps out. *100 Shot/100 Killed* did it first, as it turns out. There is a scene where a villain jumps out of a plane with Hoshino handcuffed and helpless inside.

Yumi and Detective Tezuka (comedic actor Ichiro Arishima, the Charlie Chaplin of Japan and Mr. Tako in *King Kong vs. Godzilla*) show up to rescue him. Specifically, Yumi pilots another plane directly over Hoshino's. They drop out a ladder connecting the two planes and Tezuka climbs down into Hoshino's plane! No actual dangerous mid-air stuntwork was attempted as the Bond films might have done (and later did in films like *Octopussy*) but it's still well done. Tezuka manages to take over the controls and save Hoshino while Yumi takes aim at the villain, who jumped from the plane in his parachute. It's rather shocking for a light-hearted

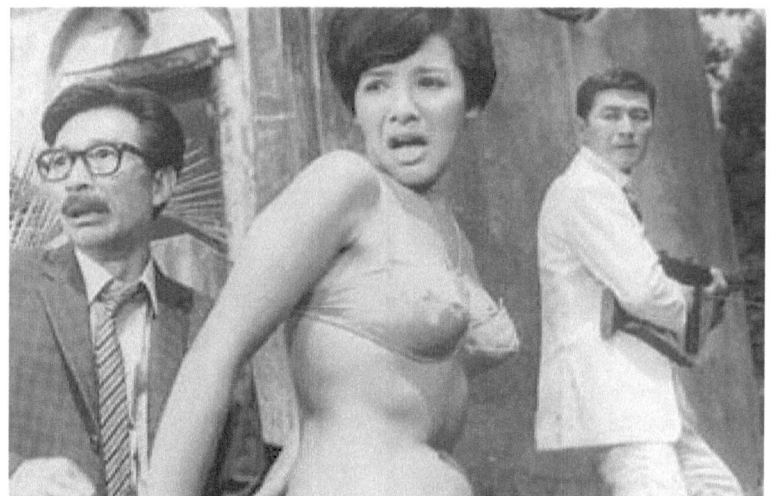

Above: Ichiro Arishima, Mie Hama and Takarada in IRONFINGER. Right: Italian poster touting Hama as the star. 100 SHOT/100 KILLED © 1965 TOHO CO.,

spoof, but Yumi rams her plane into the parachuting villain causing a cascade of blood to obscure her windshield! (This scene would likely have been edited out of a U.S. release had it gotten one.)

Yumi parachutes out of her plane, which can no longer run due to what she's just done. Meanwhile, Tezuka and Hoshino have become the prisoners of Du Bois, the main villain who's finally made his appearance. (Before this, the film was lacking a solid main villain.) The following sequence plays out like a less grand version of *Dr. No* due to the tropical setting. While Hoshino and Tezuka are being held in a jail cell, Yumi pops up outside the window. She is wearing a plastic explosive laced bikini and ready to rescue them! Though her rescue works and they manage to escape, they are eventually recaptured.

Similar to the Bond films in which 007 escapes certain death before an execution, the same thing happens here when the heroes face a firing squad. They give a final request (cigarettes) which Du-Bois honors being French. They then

toss the matches given to them at some oil drums causing an explosion and chaos ensues allowing them to escape. All three get their hands on some assault rifles and go to town on the villains.

The film's epilogue is interesting in that we still don't get confirmation as to who "Andrew Hoshino" really is. This isn't the writers incompetence though, the film deliberately toys with us, as Tezuka practically begs "Hoshino" to tell him who he really is. Instead, Hoshino boards a motorboat and leaves the island.

Many critics have noted that the Bond films often end with 007 romancing the female lead near a large body of water. It is the same here. Yumi, who Hoshino tried to leave behind, was secretly clinging behind the boat the whole time and begins to water ski! Eventually she falls into the ocean, but Hoshino stops the boat and jumps in after her. There, an underwater flirtation commences—and this was filmed at the same time as *Thunderball*, so it's unlikely it was able to influence the scene here. In a humorous scene, Hoshino breaks the fourth wall and more or less tells we, the audience, to get lost so he and Yumi can have some alone time.

100 SHOT/100 KILLED: GOLDENEYE

Release Date: March 16, 1968
Alternate Titles: BOOTED BABE, BUSTED BOSS (International)

DIRECTED BY: Jun Fukuda SCREENPLAY BY: Ei Ogawa, Jun Fukuda & Michio Tsuzuki MUSIC BY: Masaru Sato CAST: Akira Takarada (Andrew Hoshino) Beverly Maeda (Ruby) Tomomi Sawa (Mitsuko Saitô) Andrew Hughes (Stonefeller) Makoto Satô (Lt. Tezuka) Yoshio Tsuchiya (Kurokawa)

Tohoscope, Eastmancolor, 80 Minutes

Either while on vacation or perhaps on assignment in Beirut, Andrew Hoshino crosses paths with an orphan girl. Her father was killed by an assassin named Kurokawa. The girl offers Hoshino a simple silver dollar as payment to avenge her father, and he is touched enough to take on the job.

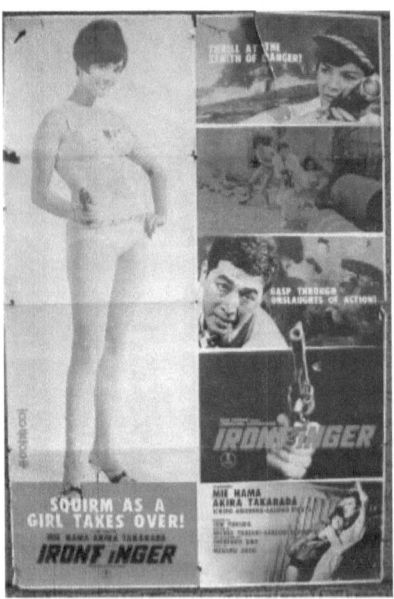

THE LOST FILMS FANZINE PRESENTS MOVIE MILESTONES #5

100 SHOT/100 KILLED : GOLDENEYE® 1967 TOHO CO., LTD

As it turns out, the simple silver dollar is actually a very valuable gold coin in disguise, and holds the key to exposing a corrupt gold smuggling syndicate run by a man named Stonefeller. The coin falls into the possesion of a female race car driver who Hoshino then has to rescue. Aiding him is another beautiful assassin named Ruby. Togehter, Hoshino and Ruby take down Kurokawa and Stonefeller both.

OVERVIEW: Like all sequels, this one is much zanier than the first and is pure Sixties pop. There's Arabic assassins pushing machine-gun stocked baby carriages, a helicopter with a deadly grappling hook, a female pop singer who doubles as a race car driver, the list goes on. Toho bit player Andrew Hughes (the older Caucasian gentleman seen in movies like 1968's *Destroy All Monsters* and 1974's *ESPY*) gets a bigger than usual role in this one as the big boss. Like Blofeld, the famous Bond villain, when we first "meet" Stonefeller, we never see his face. We can only hear him as he sits behind a desk, and instead of a pussy cat he has a rather intimidating dog. As it later turns out, this is his seeing-eye dog as he's blind. Though he's blind, he's still a deadly assassin by way of a special rifle, with a directional microphone attached to it. At the film's end, he hunts Hoshino in the darkness by sound. Overall, he's an improvement over the last film's villain (at least in terms of cool gimmicks).

While Mie Hama is indeed missed (still wish she coulda got a spinoff!) Beverly Maeda is nearly just a fun as the female assassin Ruby. (If you'll recall, Maeda played jungle girl Saeko in 1967's *Son of Godzilla*). Like Thomas Milian's Cuchillo character (*Run Man, Run!*), Ruby can throw a knife quicker than most men can draw a gun. Unfortunately she only uses this trick once though, and coming early on in the film one assumes this will be her gimmick though ultimately it's not. (She doesn't really have a gim-

73

mick, by the way, which makes her a bit inferior to Hama's character).

More false expectations come from the great Yoshio Tsuchiya (famous to monster fans as the head aliens in *The Mysterians* and *Invasion of Astro-Monster*). He kicks off the film's pre-credit scene by chasing down a man in a helicopter, violently impaling him with a grappling hook attached to the chopper. In a way, he's Akihiko Hirata's replacement as the deadly henchman, though he meets his end midway through the film. (It would've been nice if he had served as the final boss, so to speak.)

Takarada is delightful as always, but his performance in the previous film was more fun. In that one, for a while at least, you weren't sure if Hoshino might actually be a momma's boy turned assassin. This film finally reveals that M.O.M. is the codename of the organization that Hoshino works for, hence his always referring to Momma!

Fukuda's direction is well-done yet again, though this film is a notch below its predecessor. There's not quite as much inventive action this time around compared to the first entry. The film also contains a car chase in the country that is something between a similar scene from *For Your Eyes Only* (1981) and the car chase Fukuda directed for *Godzilla vs. Megalon* (1973).

Sato's score is a bit more jazzy this time and less similar to the one he composed for *Ebirah, Horror of the Deep*. That said, the go-go dance-athon music Sato composed for *Ebirah* returns here as radio music that Hoshino and Ruby dance to in their hotel room.

It's tough to say why the *100 Shot/100 Killed* series didn't continue after this entry. It could be that it wasn't a hit at the box office, or it could have just been that the spy craze was finally beginning to subside. By the time that 1971's *Diamonds Are Forever* re-invigorated the genre, Toho had disbanded their old studio system, and actors like Akira Takarada and Mie Hama were no longer under contract there.

Though neither of the *100 Shot* films have seen a licensed home video release in the U.S., the films have at least been subtitled and are currently screening on the Criterion Channel if you'd like to check them out.

THE UNMADE FILES: 100 SHOT/100 KILLED: BIG DUEL IN THE SOUTH SEAS In the book EIJI TSUBURAYA: MASTER OF MONSTERS, on page 144, it is written that KING KONG VS. EBIRAH was "retooled and combined with another shelved script, a proposed Akira Takarada vehicle, 100 SHOT/100 KILLED: BIG DUEL IN THE SOUTH SEAS a follow-up to the 1965 Jun Fukuda hit, 100 SHOT/100 KILLED." If this is true, we could then gather that there was an unmade sequel where Andrew Hoshino found himself stranded on an island where a communist military group has built a nuclear weapons base. This doesn't seem hard to believe, as EBIRAH feels like a spy movie at times. In any case, it would have been quite fun to see Hoshino square off against Hirata's eye-patch wearing commander!

THE LOST FILMS FANZINE PRESENTS MOVIE MILESTONES #5

THE BICEP BOOKS CATALOGUE

The following titles are available for purchase on Amazon.com, and are available to bookstores at a wholesale discount via Ingram Content Group (ISBNs of available editions listed for this purpose)

THE BIG BOOK OF JAPANESE GIANT MONSTER MOVIES SERIES

The third edition of the book that started it all! Reviews over 100 tokusatsu films between 1954 and 1988. All the Godzilla, Gamera, and Daimajin movies made during the Showa era are covered plus lesser known fare like *Invisible Man vs. The Human Fly* (1957) and *Conflagration* (1975). Softcover (380 pp/5.83" X 8.27") Suggested Retail: $19.99 SBN:978-1-7341546-4-1

This third edition reviews over 75 tokusatsu films between 1989 and 2019. All the Godzilla, Gamera, and Ultraman movies made during the Heisei era are covered plus independent films like *Reigo, King of the Sea Monsters* (2005), *Demeking, the Sea Monster* (2009) and *Attack of the Giant Teacher* (2019)! Softcover (260 pp/5.83" X 8.27") Suggested Retail: $19.99 ISBN: 978-1-7347816-4-9

This second edition of the Rondo Award nominated book covers un-produced scripts like *Bride of Godzilla* (1955), partially shot movies like *Giant Horde Beast Nezura* (1963), and banned films like *Prophecies of Nostradamus* (1974), plus hundreds of other lost productions. Softcover/Hard-cover (470pp, /7" X 10") Suggested Retail: $24.99 (sc)/$39.95(hc)ISBN: 978-1-7341546-0-3 (hc)

This sequel to *The Lost Films* covers the non-giant monster unmade movie scripts from Japan such as *Frankenstein vs. the Human Vapor* (1963), *After Japan Sinks* (1974-76), plus lost movies like *Fearful Attack of the Flying Saucers* (1956) and *Venus Flytrap* (1968). Hardcover (200 pp/5.83" X 8.27")/Softcover (216 pp/ 5.5" X 8.5") Suggested Retail: $9.99 (sc)/$24.99(hc)   ISBN:978-1-7341546-3-4 (hc)

This companion book to *The Lost Films* charts the development of all the prominent Japanese monster movies including discarded screenplays, story ideas, and deleted scenes. Also includes bios for writers like Shinichi Sekizawa, Niisan Takahashi and many others. Comprehensive script listing and appendices as well. Hardcover/Softcover (370 pp./ 6"X9") Suggested Retail: $16.95(sc)/$34.99(hc)ISBN: 978-1-7341546-5-8 (hc)

Examines the differences between the U.S. and Japanese versions of over 50 different tokusatsu films like *Gojira* (1954)/*Godzilla, King of the Monsters!* (1956), *Gamera* (1965)/ *Gammera, the Invincible* (1966), *Submersion of Japan* (1973)/*Tidal Wave* (1975), and many, many more! Softcover (540 pp./ 6"X9") Suggested Retail: $22.99(sc) ISBN: 978-1-953221-77-3

This second volume examines the differences between the European and Japanese versions of tokusatsu films including the infamous "Cozzilla" colorized version of *Godzilla, King of the Monsters!* from 1977, plus rarities like *Terremoto 10 Grado*, the Italian cut of *Legend of Dinosaurs*. The book also examines the condensed Champion Matsuri edits of Toho's effects films. Coming 2022.

Throughout the 1960s and 1970s the Italian film industry cranked out over 600 "Spaghetti Westerns" and for every *Fistful of Dollars* were a dozen pale imitations, some of them hilarious. Many of these lesser known Spaghettis are available in bargain bin DVD packs and stream for free online. If ever you've wondered which are worth your time and which aren't, this is the book for you. Softcover (160pp./5.06" X 7.8") Suggested Retail: $9.99

75

THE LOST FILMS FANZINE PRESENTS MOVIE MILESTONES #5

THE BICEP BOOKS CATALOGUE

CLASSIC MONSTERS SERIES

Kong Unmade explores unproduced scripts like *King Kong vs. Frankenstein* (1958), unfinished films like *The Lost Island* (1934), and lost movies like *King Kong Appears in Edo* (1938). As a bonus, all the Kong rip-offs like *Konga* (1961) and *Queen Kong* (1976) are reviewed. Hardcover (350 pp/5.83" X 8.27")/Softcover (376 pp/ 5.5" X 8.5") Suggested Retail: $24.99 (hc)/$19.99(sc) ISBN: 978-1-7341546-2-7(hc)

Jaws Unmade explores unproduced scripts like *Jaws 3, People 0* (1979), abandoned ideas like a Quint prequel, and even aborted sequels to Jaws inspired movies like *Orca Part II*. As a bonus, all the Jaws rip-offs like *Grizzly* (1976) and *Tentacles* (1977) are reviewed. Hardcover (316 pp/5.83" X 8.27")/Softcover (340 pp/5.5" X 8.5") Suggested Retail: $29.99 (hc)/$17.95(sc) ISBN: 978-1-7344730-1-8

Classic Monsters Unmade covers lost and unmade films starring Dracula, Frankenstein, the Mummy and more monsters. Reviews unmade scripts like *The Return of Frankenstein* (1934) and *Wolf Man vs. Dracula* (1944). It also examines lost films of the silent era such as *The Werewolf* (1913) and *Drakula's Death* (1923). Softcover/Hardcover(428pp/5.83"X8.27") Suggested Retail: $22.99(sc)/$27.99(hc)ISBN:978-1-953221-85-8(hc)

Volume 2 explores the Hammer era and beyond, from unmade versions of *Brides of Dracula* (called *Disciple of Dracula*) to remakes of *Creature from the Black Lagoon*. Completely unmade films like *Kali: Devil Bride of Dracula* (1975) and *Godzilla vs. Frankenstein* (1964) are covered along with lost completed films like *Batman Fights Dracula* (1967) and *Black the Ripper* (1974). Coming Fall 2021.

NOSTALGIA

Written in the same spirit as *The Big Book of Japanese Giant Monster Movies*, this tome reviews all the classic Universal and Hammer horrors to star Dracula, Frankenstein, the Gillman and the rest along with obscure flicks like *The New Invisible Man* (1958), *Billy the Kid versus Dracula* (1966), *Blackenstein* (1973) and *Legend of the Werewolf* (1974). Coming 2021.

Written at an intermediate reading level for the kid in all of us, these picture books will take you back to your youth. In the spirit of the old Ian Thorne books are covered *Nabonga* (1944), *White Pongo* (1945) and more! Hardcover/Softcover (44 pp/7.5" X 9.25") Suggested Retail: $17.95(hc)/$9.99(sc) ISBN: 978- 1-7341546-9-6 (hc) 978- 1-7344730-5-6 (sc)

Written at an intermediate reading level for the kid in all of us, these picture books will take you back to your youth. In the spirit of the old Ian Thorne books are covered *The Lost World* (1925), *The Land That Time Forgot* (1975) and more! Hardcover/Softcover (44 pp/7.5" X 9.25") Suggested Retail: $17.95 (hc)/$9.99(sc) ISBN: 978-1-7344730 -6-3 (hc) 978- 1-7344730-7-0 (sc)

Written at an intermediate reading level for the kid in all of us, these picture books will take you back to your youth. In the spirit of the old Ian Thorne books are covered *Them!* (1954), *Empire of the Ants* (1977) and more! Hardcover/Softcover (44 pp/7.5" X 9.25") Suggested Retail: $17.95(hc)/$9.99(sc) ISBN: 978-1-7347816 -3-2 (hc) 978 -1-7347816-2-5 (sc)

THE LOST FILMS FANZINE PRESENTS MOVIE MILESTONES #5

THE BICEP BOOKS CATALOGUE

CRYPTOZOOLOGY/COWBOYS & SAURIANS

Cowboys & Saurians: Prehistoric Beasts as Seen by the Pioneers explores dinosaur sightings from the pioneer period via real newspaper reports from the time. Well-known cases like the Tombstone Thunderbird are covered along with more obscure cases like the Crosswicks Monster and more. Softcover (357 pp/5.06" X 7.8") Suggested Retail: $19.95 ISBN: 978-1-7341546-1-0

Cowboys & Saurians: Ice Age zeroes in on snowbound saurians like the Ceratosaurus of the Arctic Circle and a Tyrannosaurus of the Tundra, as well as sightings of Ice Age megafauna like mammoths, glyptodonts, Sarkastodons and Sabertoothed tigers. Tales of a land that time forgot in the Arctic are also covered. Softcover (264 pp/5.06" X 7.8") Suggested Retail: $14.99 ISBN: 978-1-7341546-7-2

Southerners & Saurians takes the series formula of exploring newspaper accounts of monsters in the pioneer period with an eye to the Old South. In addition to dinosaurs are covered Lizardmen, Frogmen, giant leeches and mosquitoes, and the Dingocroc, which might be an alien rather than a prehistoric survivor. Softcover (202 pp/5.06" X 7.8") Suggested Retail: $13.99 ISBN: 978-1-7344730-4-9

Cowboys & Saurians: South of the Border explores the saurians of Central and South America, like the Patagonian Plesiosaurus that was really an Iemisch, plus tales of the Neo-Mylodon (a giant ground sloth), a menacing monster from underground called the Minhocao, Glyptodonts, shark-men and even a three-headed dinosaur! Coming Summer 2021 ISBN: 978-1-953221-73-5

UFOLOGY/THE REAL COWBOYS & ALIENS IN CONJUNCTION WITH ROSWELL BOOKS

The Real Cowboys and Aliens: Early American UFOs explores UFO sightings in the USA between the years 1800-1864. Stories of encounters sometimes involved famous figures in U.S. history such as Lewis and Clark, and Thomas Jefferson.Hardcover (242pp/6" X 9") Softcover (262 pp/5.06" X 7.8") Suggested Retail: $24.99 (hc)/$15.95(sc) ISBN: 978-1-7341546-8-9\(hc)/978-1-7344730-8-7(sc)

The second entry in the series, *Old West UFOs*, covers reports spanning the years 1865-1895. Includes tales of Men in Black, Reptilians, Spring-Heeled Jack, Sasquatch from space, and other alien beings, in addition to the UFOs and airships. Hardcover (276 pp/6" X 9") Softcover (308 pp/5.06" X 7.8") Suggested Retail: $29.95 (hc)/$17.95(sc) ISBN: 978-1-7344730-0-1 (hc)/ 978-1-7344730-2-5 (sc)

The third entry in the series, *The Coming of the Airships*, encompasses a short time frame with an incredibly high concentration of airship sightings between 1896-1899. The famous Aurora, Texas, UFO crash of 1897 is covered in depth along with many others. Hardcover (196 pp/6" X 9") Softcover (222 pp/5.06" X 7.8") Suggested Retail: $24.99 (hc)/$15.95(sc) ISBN: 978-1-7347816 -1-8 (hc)/978-1-7347816-0-1(sc)

Early 20th Century UFOs kicks off a new series that investigates UFO sightings of the early 1900s. Includes tales of UFOs sighted over the Titanic as it sank, Nikola Tesla receiving messages from the stars, an alien being found encased in ice, and a possible virus from outer space!Hardcover (196 pp/6" X 9") Softcover (222 pp/5.06" X 7.8") Suggested Retail: $27.99 (hc)/$16.95(sc) ISBN: 978-1-7347816-1-8 (hc)/978-1-7347816-0-1(sc)

BACK ISSUES

THE LOST FILMS FANZINE

ISSUE #1 SPRING 2020 The lost Italian cut of *Legend of Dinosaurs and Monster Birds* called *Terremoto 10 Grado*, plus *Bride of Dr. Phibes* script, *Good Luck! Godzilla*, the King Kong remake that became a car comm ercial, Bollywood's lost *Jaws* rip-off, Top Ten Best Fan Made Godzilla trailers plus an interview with Scott David Lister. 60 pages. Three variant covers/editions (premium color/basic color/b&w)

ISSUE #2 SUMMER 2020 How 1935's *The Capture of Tarzan* became 1936's *Tarzan Escapes*, the Orca sequels that weren't, Baragon in Bollywood's *One Million B.C.*, unmade *Kolchak: The Night Stalker* movies, *The Norliss Tapes*, *Superman V: The New Movie*, why there were no *Curse of the Pink Panther* sequels, *Moonlight Mask: The Movie*. 64 pages. Two covers/editions (basic color/b&w)

ISSUE #3 FALL 2020 Blob sequels both forgotten and unproduced, *Horror of Dracula* uncut, Frankenstein Meets the Wolfman and talks, myths of the lost *King Kong* Spider-Pit sequence debunked, the *Carnosaur* novel vs. the movies, *Terror in the Streets* 50th anniversary, *Bride of Godzilla* 55th Unniversary, Lee Powers sketchbook. 100 pages. Two covers/editions (basic color/b&w)

ISSUE #4 WINTER 2020/21 *Diamonds Are Forever's* first draft with Goldfinger, *Disciple of Dracula* into *Brides of Dracula*, *War of the Worlds That Weren't Part II*, *Day the Earth Stood Still II* by Ray Bradbury, *Deathwish 6*, *Atomic War Bride*, *What Am I Doing in the Middle of a Revolution?*, *Spring Dream in the Old Capital* and more. 70 pages. Two covers/editions (basic color/b&w)

MOVIE MILESTONES

ISSUE #1 AUGUST 2020 Debut issue celebrating 80 years of *One Million B.C.* (1940), and an early 55th Anniversary for *One Million Years B.C.* (1966). Abandoned ideas, casting changes, and deleted scenes are covered, plus, a mini-B.C. stock-footage filmography and much more! 54 pages. Three collectible covers/editions (premium color/ basic color/b&w)

ISSUE #2 OCTOBER 2020 Celebrates the joint 50th Anniversaries of *When Dinosaurs Ruled the Earth* (1970) and *Creatures the World Forgot* (1971). Also includes looks at *Prehistoric Women* (1967), *When Women Had Tails* (1970), and *Caveman* (1981), plus unmade films like *When the World Cracked Open*. 72 pages. Three collectible covers/editions (premium color/basic color/b&w)

ISSUE #3 WINTER 2021 Japanese 'Panic Movies' like *The Last War* (1961), *Submersion of Japan* (1973), and *Bullet Train* (1975) are covered on celebrated author Sakyo Komatsu's 90th birthday. The famous banned Toho film *Prophecies of Nostradamus* (1974) are also covered. 124 pages. Three collectible covers/editions (premium color/ basic color/ b&w)

ISSUE #4 SPRING 2021 This issue celebrates the joint 60th Anniversaries of *Gorgo*, *Reptilicus* and *Konga* examining unmade sequels like *Reptilicus 2*, and other related lost projects like *Kuru Island* and *The Volcano Monsters*. Also explores the Gorgo, Konga and Reptilicus comic books from Charlton. 72 pages. Three collectible covers/editions (premium color/basic color/b&w)

44577CB00002B/349